Bit Player

Bit Player

My Life with Presidents and Ideas

Stephen Hess

Brookings Institution Press
Washington, D.C.

The Brookings Institution is a private nonprofit organization devoted to research, education, and publication on important issues of domestic and foreign policy. Its principal purpose is to bring the highest quality independent research and analysis to bear on current and emerging policy problems. Interpretations or conclusions in Brookings publications should be understood to be solely those of the authors.

Library of Congress Cataloging-in-Publication data are available.
ISBN 978-0-8157-3699-8 (cloth : alk. paper)
ISBN 978-0-8157-3700-1 (ebook)

9 8 7 6 5 4 3 2 1

Typeset in Adobe Garamond Pro

Composition by Elliott Beard

To my parents, Florence and Charles Hess,
whose enveloping love is the deepest memory
of my childhood

I've been repaid a thousand times over with adventures, with good company, and with the satisfaction of serving something more important than myself, of being a bit player in the extraordinary story of America. And I am so very grateful.

—JOHN MCCAIN, *October 16, 2017*

Contents

Foreword   xiii

Preface   xvii

Eisenhower   1

First Words   4
Getting There   6
First Politics, 1952   10
Enter Professor Moos   13
Drafted   17
The Eisenhower White House, 1958–61   19
The Staff   23
The 1960 Election   28
Speeches   35
Remembering Ike   44

Nixon   49

Interregnum, 1961   51
The Harlow Miracle   52
Working for Richard Nixon   57
California, 1962   60
November 22, 1963   73
A Bookmaker   75
Lincoln Week, 1966   80
Harvard, 1967–68   82
Miami Beach, 1968   85
The 1968 Campaign and Spiro T. Agnew   89
Deputy Assistant to the President for Urban Affairs   95
To HEW   102
The White House Conference on Children   103
A White House Conference on Youth   109
What Next?   116
Leave-Taking, 1972   118

Brookings   121

Settling In   124
Governmental Studies   127
Things to Do   130
Watergate   131
Talk   135
The Presidency Book   138
Newswork   140
Transitions   146

Beth's List: A Summing Up   153

September 11, 2001   156
Des Moines, Iowa, 1976   158
Kansas City, 1976   159

United Nations, 1974 and 1976   159
Make-A-Wish Foundation   162
Campaign Etiquette   163
Political Cartoons   164
The Notorious RBG   166
Hyman Rickover, "Father of the Nuclear Navy," 1954   168
Jacqueline Kennedy Onassis, 1977   170
Richard Avedon, 1990   171
Oliver Stone, 1994   172
Former British Prime Minister John Major, 2009   173
Circles within Circles   174

Afterword   179

Thanks   181

Index   185

Foreword

Although the title of his book is *Bit Player,* Steve Hess is anything but that in the history of the Brookings Institution. Steve joined Brookings in 1972 as one of just five senior fellows in the Brookings Governmental Studies program and has been an integral part of the institution ever since. He's a regular fixture at both public and private events, as well as at informal meetings and discussions around the institution. A prolific author, Steve has published seventeen books with the Brookings Institution Press and has so many stories to tell that the Brookings Cafeteria podcast once featured a long-running series of "Steve Hess Stories." That is only a small taste of the tremendous legacy Steve has built at Brookings and an even smaller example of his importance as a true public servant throughout his many years in and around government.

Bit Player: My Life with Presidents and Ideas is as enjoyable for its tales of remarkable encounters with the likes of Jacqueline Kennedy Onassis and Ruth Bader Ginsburg as it is for its first-person account of Brookings history. Steve recalls how the beloved Brookings Friday Lunch tradition came to be, and recounts the time after an early installment of the lunch series when Harvard professor Samuel Beer remarked, "At the Harvard Faculty Club we note a pleasant meal and go back to our offices. Here you get up from the table and declare, 'What are we going to do about it!'" If that isn't a perfect depiction of the Brookings Institution spirit, I don't know what is.

And to that end, no one could ever doubt that Steve is a person who does something "about it"—no matter what "it" is. His accomplishments are as diverse as they are impressive, and the breadth of knowledge and experience he has gained in the course of his career has been applied to his scholarship at Brookings for the past forty-six years. Some of the remarkable highlights from that career include serving as a member of the White House staff under Presidents Eisenhower and Nixon, as an adviser to Presidents Ford and Carter, and as U.S. representative to the United Nations General Assembly and the UNESCO General Conference. Additionally, Steve chaired the White House Conferences on Children and Youth, served on the District of Columbia's Board of Higher Education, and was even named to *Time* magazine's list of "200 Young American Leaders" in 1974. *Time* couldn't have been more right to put him on that list, and we're incredibly proud of Steve's many, many achievements.

Not just a reflection on a life well lived (though it is certainly that), *Bit Player* is also a powerful reminder of how much we can learn from the past and from the experiences of others. Steve's accounting of the Watergate scandal and his own shock at learning the truth about his friend and boss Richard Nixon is refreshingly honest, especially when read in the context of today's political tribalism and accusations of "fake news." "I was dead wrong," he writes about his efforts to explain how the Watergate crimes could have happened without Nixon's knowledge. How much better off would we be if more people were willing to survey their past or currently held convictions and admit they might have been wrong!

Bit Player is a hopeful book that paints an optimistic picture about the Washington in which Hess has resided for so long. He demonstrates to his readers—with firsthand accounts—that many of the officials who have led this country over the past fifty-plus years, either in the public eye or behind the scenes, have cared deeply about their country and their fellow citizens. Beginning with his tales from the White House Mess during the Eisenhower years, straight through to the time he opened his home to a group of displaced State Department officials and British parliamentarians on September 11, 2001, Steve brings to life a Washington full of dedicated and committed public servants.

Brookings, in its more than 100 years of existence as an American public policy institution, has been blessed to have many exceptional leaders pass through its halls, both as guests and as staff. Among those, few can match Steve's magnificent array of accomplishments, his dedication to public service, and, most cherished by us, his passion and love for this institution. We are a better organization because of Steve's efforts over the years and are deeply appreciative of the excellent book he's written. I hope you enjoy the book, and to Steve: Thank you for all you've done for Brookings!

John R. Allen
President, Brookings Institution

Preface

To be helpful, I have my résumé translated into Greek for a talk I am to give in Athens.

I offer it to the professor who is to introduce me. "What is your title at Brookings, Mr. Hess?" he asks.

"Senior Fellow," I reply.

"It has been translated 'Ancient Gentleman.'"

———

In the 1940s and 1950s, Upton Sinclair—the Pulitzer Prize–winning author of *The Jungle*—wrote eleven best-selling novels featuring a character named Lanny Budd. They were works of fiction—Lanny was not real, of course, nor was he famous or of high rank. But whenever an important political event was happening somewhere, Lanny also happened to be there. Now, as an ancient gentleman, the more I remember, the more I feel I have lived a Lanny Budd life:

1952: Chicago, I am nineteen, and on the convention floor as Dwight Eisenhower and Robert Taft are deadlocked for the Republican presidential nomination. . . . 1958: Washington, I am twenty-five, writing speeches for President Eisenhower during the disastrous midterm election. . . . 1960: New York, Richard Nixon secretly negotiates the so-called Compact of Fifth Avenue with Nelson Rockefeller for the Republican platform; in Chicago, I listen by phone to what they are instructing platform chair Charles Percy. . . . 1959–1961: Washington, on the White House speechwriting team. Ike delivers his farewell address. . . . 1962: Los Angeles, I am Nixon's speechwriter as he runs for California governor. . . . 1963: November 22, President Kennedy is assassinated in Dallas; I am with Nixon. . . . 1965: Washington, Gerald Ford is elected leader of the House Republicans. I begin writing speeches for him. . . . 1968: Miami, Nixon chooses Spiro Agnew for vice president. I travel 60,000 gaffe-filled miles with him on the campaign trail. . . . 1969: On the White House staff again, as liberals and conservatives battle for President Nixon's attention; I am Pat Moynihan's deputy. . . . 1973: October 20, a quiet dinner with Tom and Meredith Brokaw ends abruptly with what becomes known as the Saturday Night Massacre. . . . 1976: Kansas City, I am editor in chief of President Ford's platform. . . . 1976: New York, November 19, I am a delegate to the UN General Assembly, on leave from Brookings, when President-elect Carter calls to ask for help organizing the White House. . . . Washington, November 20, Saturday morning, I am in the West Wing reviewing staffing charts with Ford's chief of staff, Dick Cheney. . . . 1980: The Republican national chairman asks me to write a Reagan transition plan. . . .

Eisenhower

On August 16, 1958, the *General Alexander M. Patch* debarked at the Brooklyn Army Terminal. Back from Germany, I was on my way to Fort Dix, New Jersey, where my two-year military career—during which I rose from private to private first class—was to end some nine days later. Someday I will claim that my replacement in the 3rd Armored Division was Elvis Presley, which is almost true—at least in the sense that his unit moved in when my unit moved out.

I was twenty-five, about to be unemployed, and available.

On September 1, President Eisenhower's speechwriter, Arthur Larson, resigns. Unknown to me, his successor will be Malcolm Moos, my professor at Johns Hopkins, who wants me to join him at the White House. I begin September 8.

When asked by students how to become a presidential speechwriter, my reply is always "Be nice to your professors." Of course, it was not quite that simple. White House chief of staff Sherman Adams is being pushed out (for accepting gifts—a vicuña coat, an oriental rug—from a favor-seeker named Bernard Goldfine). He is not willing to let the new speechwriter hire an assistant. So Moos, who has a politician's instincts, does an end run around Adams and goes to the chairman of the Republican National Committee, Mead Alcorn. Since I will be working on the president's speeches for the midterm campaign, Mac says, surely the party would be willing to foot the bill. Alcorn agrees, and I visit him on September 4. He calls me Steve. What compensation do I want? It is a question I have never been asked before. The army never asked when it made me a private. I say a thousand dollars a month. I don't know where this figure comes from. Alcorn quickly agrees. I must have asked for too little. I add: "There will be expenses." I have no idea what this means. He says they will pay for an apartment. I say: "I would like a four-month contract." He says that is fair. I am getting pretty good at this negotiating thing! The chairman says he would also like to call on me for some speeches. Fine with me. As it turns out, I end up writing only one speech and a few notes for him, including a good story about Teddy Roosevelt for him to use at TR's centennial. What I think happens is that my working at the White House intimidates the RNC.

Three weeks after my ship docked, I am in Washington, writing speeches for the president of the United States, for $1,000 a month in 1958 dollars, which works out to an annual salary of $102,014 in 2018 dollars. And I have an apartment in Georgetown. Is this just a series of interesting accidents? Where does the story go from here?

First Words

September 25, 1958: I write in my diary, "If there are no changes, tomorrow will be the first time the President speaks any of my words."

There was to be a ceremony on the restoration of Fort Ligonier in western Pennsylvania, a frontier post during the French and Indian War. George Washington fought there in 1758. President Eisenhower's visit was a favor to billionaire Richard Mellon. The speeches—by Ike, Mellon, and a senator—lasted just eighteen minutes, followed by a twenty-minute visit to Mellon's 30,000-acre estate, then back to the White House by 5:58 p.m.

My assignment was to thread a connection between Washington and

Eisenhower, the two "war hero" presidents. What I learned was that Colonel Washington's troops had circled the fort clockwise in heavy fog while another young officer from Virginia circled his troops counterclockwise. They met, but mistook each other for the enemy: two officers and thirty-eight enlisted men were killed or wounded. Recounting George Washington's "friendly fire" incident did not seem the most auspicious way to begin my career as a speechwriter at the White House.

All that survived of my draft was one sentence: "Thanks to the public interest of many citizens, a large part of this historic site has been restored, so that today we see it much as it must have appeared to young Colonel Washington 200 years ago."

Actually . . .

That was not the first speech I ever wrote for a major public figure. In 1954, as a student at Johns Hopkins University in Baltimore, I went to Washington for the day to see if I might pick up some useful information for a paper I was writing on the Bricker Amendment, a controversial effort by right-wingers to amend the Constitution to place restrictions on the president's treaty-making powers. It seems quaint by the standards of today's overdriven Congress, but I actually walked into the office of Minnesota senator Hubert Humphrey, politely stated my request, and was introduced to Max Kampelman, his top legislative assistant. Max not only told me about the ins and outs of Senate strategy but wanted to know *my* opinion of the Bricker Amendment. At the end of our conversation, he asked me—words to be remembered—"Would you write the senator's speech?" Wow! Humphrey's speech, Hess-written, is in the *Congressional Record*, February 3, 1954, starting on page 1229. There was one way I could prove to my friends that I was really the author: I wrote my name into the speech! Max introduced me to other senators' aides and volunteered my services. I was particularly grateful to draft a speech for a family favorite, Herbert Lehman of New York, who bore a strong physical resemblance to my late father. Several weeks later I returned to Washington and asked Max if I could see the reaction to the speech. He took me into the senator's office, seated me at the senator's desk, and brought in a file. The first letter was from a man who found fault in that his organization was not in a list of groups opposing the Bricker Amendment. Humphrey's response was "Sorry, the speech was written by a volunteer."

Max Kampelman died at the age of ninety-three in 2013. After he left Senator Humphrey's office, his career as a prominent Washington attorney included major diplomatic assignments. In 1999 President Clinton awarded him the Presidential Medal of Freedom. I am proud that he remained my friend for life.

Getting There

There are footprints, at least on my mother's side, of a family fascination with politics and public service.

My Aunt Rose, whom I remember drinking tea in the kitchen with my mother when I was a little boy, was my mother's aunt, Rose Livingston, known in the New York press as the "Angel of Chinatown" for her work rescuing young white and Chinese girls from forced prostitution. My mother's uncle, Henry Moskowitz, ran for Congress in 1912 on Teddy Roosevelt's Progressive Party ticket and was a founder of the NAACP. His wife, Belle, managed Democrat Alfred E. Smith's campaign for president in 1928. Herbert Hoover, the Republican, won in a landslide, yet the *New York Times* credited Belle with being "nearer than any woman had come before to being the maker of a President." I never met Belle, who died before I was born, but when I was three my mother took me to visit Uncle Henry, who autographed a large studio portrait, which my mother hung in my bedroom. If Florence Hess was wishing for subliminal influence, here it is: Uncle Henry wrote Al Smith's campaign biography—and forty years later her son wrote one for another presidential candidate, Richard Nixon.

The only grandparent I knew, Max Morse (he changed his name from Moskowitz), was a disappointing father to my mother but a great grandfather to me. When selling women's coats, he would arrange to arrive in any city west of Manhattan—Cincinnati, St. Louis, Chicago—

when the Giants had an important game. Baseball was his passion and his legacy to his grandson. In the 1970s he lived in a decaying hotel on Broadway, the Ansonia, where visiting teams were lodged and where he spent evenings chatting in the lobby with bored players. He gave me a large collection of scorecards—and some autographs, possibly forged by him. Together we went to the Old Timers' games at the Polo Grounds and Yankee Stadium, and I even met Babe Ruth. (No, I can't find his autograph.) What I remember was how scared I was of the croak that was Babe's voice. He was dying of cancer and his larynx had been removed.

My father, Charles Hess, was born in Baltimore in 1891. His father was listed in the 1900 Baltimore census as an expressman: he had a horse and wagon and moved things for a price. Some years ago, after I gave a luncheon talk, a friendly woman in the audience, Rita Margolis, introduced herself as a relative on my father's side and presented me with a genealogy tracing my roots back 250 years, to a little town fifty-five miles south of Warsaw. My dad, though wondrously bright, never went to school beyond the fifth or sixth grade. In his teens he invented a shorthand system while working as a stenographer in an engineering company. He devoured newspapers, surely another piece of my legacy; living in New York, we awoke with the *Times*; the *World Telegram* came home in the evening with my father from work. My mother, a Democrat, added the *Post*. They were a mixed marriage politically. He said he was the only person he knew who voted for Alf Landon, the 1936 Republican presidential candidate. On Sundays the *Times* ran a current events quiz, and it was a weekend treat to "assist" my father whip through the answers. On Sunday evenings during World War II we gathered around a large Philco in the living room to listen to the news commentaries of Gabriel Heatter and H. V. Kaltenborn. By the year I was born, 1933, Dad owned an Oldsmobile agency in the Bronx. In retrospect, I realized how clever it was of this smart young man without formal education or connections to seek a place in a new industry that would grow with his generation. Yet it was hardly without risks: people had no money to buy new cars during the Great Depression in the 1930s, nor were there cars to sell when people had money during World War II in the 1940s. By the time there were both cars and money, in the 1950s, my poor father had died.

We lived on the ninth floor of an apartment building on Broadway at 98th Street, from which I saw my first president. It was 1944, and Franklin Delano Roosevelt was running for a fourth term. He was coming down Broadway in an open car, waving. It was raining. This will go into the history books: a dying man trying to prove to the voters that he is in good health. Two blocks down Broadway at 96th Street, his car took a right turn into a garage, where the president was given a rubdown, fortified with cognac, and sent back out into the rain. He died on April 12. I was born a month after FDR's first inauguration. He was the only president of the United States for the first twelve years of my life.

Much of my life revolved around school. For the first six grades I attended the Ethical Culture School, at 64th Street and Central Park West. I got there and back on a trolley that went down the center of Broadway. Buses were a pain but trolleys were a joy, especially when they reversed direction and the operator moved from the front to the back (now the front), which meant that kids could race to sit in the unoccupied operator's seat. World War II on the home front was a glorious time to be a young American, learning the outlines of enemy planes, saving tin foil and other useful things for the war effort, writing V-mails to cheer up relatives overseas in the military. A just war. All together, we sang Harold Rome's lyrics to a tune by Shostakovich:

United Nations on the march
With flags unfurled,
Together fight for victory
A free new world.

After six grades, students of the Ethical Culture School continued on to Fieldston in the Bronx, the 242nd Street stop on the subway. I played on lots of sports teams because the school was so small and hung out in the print shop, where there was a linotype machine and a printing press. I even started a magazine I called *Phrase and Fable*, a collection of any-

The Fieldston News

BY SUBSCRIPTION

PRE ELECTION SPECIAL FIELDSTON SCHOOL, NEW YORK CITY, MONDAY, MARCH 20, 1950

Alexander, Hess, Pasternak Are Candidates For Council President In Tuesday's Election

CLIFFORD ALEXANDER

STEPHEN HESS

Now that the new constitution has been officially endorsed by the student body, it is a challenge to the incoming council to interpret and apply this piece of legislation for the greatest possible benefit to the students of Fieldston. Although the new constitution has provided the

The following suggestions are my hopes for the future in Fieldston student government:

Greater interest in council acttivities. This might be accomplished by establishing a closer relationship be-thing I could convince my classmates to give me to print. The masthead listed my "assistant" as Richard Ravitch, whose future would include serving as lieutenant governor of New York. Strange to think of our class as politicians-in-waiting, yet Clifford Alexander and I were always running for some class office until we were seniors and ran against each other for president of the student council. He won. Rereading our platforms in the *Fieldston News*, I now concede. He deserved to win. Although I got to the White House first, Cliff became secretary of the army. The third candidate, Alan Pasternak, became a scientist and one of Governor Jerry Brown's initial appointees to the California Energy Commission.

First Politics, 1952

I was always happy with what I was doing, while always anxious to move on to something that might be more exciting. I left high school in the middle of my senior year in 1951 to go to the University of Chicago, a politically overheated campus in the last days of Chancellor Robert Hutchins. On campus, I heard Alexander Kerensky, the failed Russian revolutionary, in debate; off campus, I heard a lot of folk music of the Pete Seeger variety, including one song I put together with a friend about the stockyards that began:

> *Down on the killin' floor,*
> *Covered with blood and gore,*
> *Union men can't work here anymore.*

The summer of 1952 in Chicago was also an eye-popping step into national politics when I worked—sort of—at the Republican National Convention. H. L. Mencken, the sage of Baltimore, once wrote, "There is something about a national convention that makes it as fascinating as a revival or a hanging. One sits through long sessions wishing heartily that all the delegates and alternates were dead and in hell—and then suddenly there comes a show so gaudy and hilarious, so melodramatic and obscene, so unimaginably exhilarating and preposterous that one lives a gorgeous year in an hour." And there I was, at what would be the greatest convention of my lifetime!

There was no doubt who I was for. The contest pitted Robert Taft against Dwight Eisenhower. Senator Taft was "Mr. Republican." No one had ever worked harder for his party, but he had run and lost twice for the GOP nomination. Did the party really want to take a chance on this loser? His opponent had never even been a Republican—no loser here—and besides, he had been the most popular general of World War II. In peacetime, Dwight Eisenhower had first been president—briefly—of Columbia University and had then returned to Europe in 1951 to become the first supreme commander of NATO. Senator Taft had opposed creating NATO. At its core, this was essentially what the general and the senator were all about: America's place in the world. Perhaps I was more aware than most nineteen-year-olds. The summer before I had biked with a friend through England and France. We sold our bikes when we reached the Alps and hitchhiked through Switzerland and Italy. This was a brief moment when troop ships became student ships and America's middle-class youth rushed to Europe and back on $300. The war had ended not all that long ago, and we could still see rubble from the London Blitz. At a military cemetery in France we visited the grave of my friend's cousin. We slept in youth hostels and exchanged impressions with people like us from other countries. I had a summer romance with a Canadian. One evening some Norwegian students told us about their king and his resistance to the German invasion. They appreciated the monarchy. "And so cheap. How much could old King Haakon eat?"

The specialness of the 1952 Republican National Convention was that the delegates arriving on July 7 would not know who their nominees would be until they left for home on July 9. Unlike today, only fourteen states held primaries. Other states chose to support a "favorite son" and were there to bargain. In the contest of Eisenhower versus Taft, the strategists' skills were going to determine the winner. Moreover, an estimated 71 million viewers were looking over their shoulders, for this was the first year the national conventions were broadcast live on TV, anchored on CBS by a new star, Walter Cronkite.

I was a volunteer with the New York County Republican Committee (Tom Dewey's organization), assigned to drive the delegates from their downtown hotel to the International Amphitheater at Halsted and 42nd Streets, up against the Union Stock Yards—not a great place to be when the wind was blowing from the wrong direction. The trip should have taken forty-five minutes. I did not tell anyone about my terrible sense of direction. On the first trip I got lost and my distinguished passengers—including one who was about to be appointed New York attorney general—chose to walk the last dozen blocks. I was thanked, fired, and rewarded with a set of convention tickets, so instead of working in the motor pool, I was free to parade around the convention floor (security was not what it is today), waving a placard and singing Irving Berlin's "I Like Ike / I'll shout it over a mike / Or from the highest steeple / The choice of We the People," while Taft volunteers tried to outsing us with "I'm Looking Over a Four Leaf Clover that I overlooked before."

While we were endlessly singing, the Eisenhower forces were accusing the Taft forces of stealing delegates, challenging the credentials of Georgia, Louisiana, and Texas. "Thou shalt not steal!" we chanted. From the podium, Illinois senator Everett McKinley Dirksen, speaking for Taft's side, pointed his finger down at Tom Dewey, the party's 1944 and 1948 candidate, in the Eisenhower camp. He intoned, as only Dirksen could: "We followed you before and you took us down the path to defeat." The convention hall erupted—deafening applause, deafening boos.

From the TV booth: "There's a great deal of confusion out there. There goes a fight. There's a photographer getting in trouble. I don't know who is hitting whom. Somebody got knocked down, but it's pretty hard to tell who it was. The officers were in the middle of it—they really are having a time here tonight."

It was wonderful!

Eisenhower won the seating contests and, as a result, the nomination on the first ballot.

The next day, when Richard Nixon, the controversial young senator from California about to be Ike's vice-presidential running mate, entered the hall, I was standing at the door he was about to walk through. His eyes shining and seemingly unfocused, he grabbed my hand, creating half of the first handshake of his new life. (Years later, when I was his speechwriter, I kept the secret of our first "meeting.")

Union songs or Irving Berlin: I was a kid who could sing politics left, right, or center. After the Republican convention, I even showed up at the Progressive Party convention (hosted by the heirs of Henry Wallace) because I had heard that Paul Robeson was going to sing. (He didn't.) At the door I was asked whether I wanted to be a delegate or an observer. I made the right choice.

Enter Professor Moos

The next month, August 1952, while visiting relatives in Baltimore, I read that Johns Hopkins University was starting a new program, the "Bronk Plan," a sort of work-at-your-own-speed arrangement with a topic and a professor. It sounded great. I drove over to the Homewood campus and asked if there was anyone around who would explain the possibilities of transferring. Happily, Dr. Carl Swisher, chairman of the Political Science Department, was in his office and would see me. He was a distinguished constitutional scholar and wasted no time. "Name the justices of the Supreme Court," he commanded. I did. "Name the president's cabinet." I was doing pretty well—the cabinet was not as large as it is today—until I got to the postmaster general, then in the cabinet. "He's the first civil servant to have the job," I said, "but I can't recall his name, Dr. Swisher." Dr. Swisher couldn't either! Thus was I promptly admitted to the political science program at Johns Hopkins. Could there have been a more efficient way to judge a nineteen-year-old than to ask him to name the justices of the Supreme Court?

In this way Malcolm Moos entered my life. His specialness, at least to me, was that he had two professional lives. Mac was both a political science professor and chairman of the Republican Party in Baltimore.

Moreover, he had a great capacity to share both lives with his favorite students. I helped him edit two chapters in a five-volume work on 1952 presidential nominating politics, research a history of the Republican Party—writing a first draft of everything from the death of Lincoln to the election of Cleveland—and even co-authored eight programs for National Educational Television (now PBS), which Moos and I later turned into a book, *Hats in the Ring: The Making of Presidential Candidates*.

It was by participating in Mac's political life that I got my first taste of politics outside the classroom. I biked from door to door to help him defeat a candidate for ward executive who was challenging Mac's control of the city party. I became the only paid worker in a congressional district race that was hopelessly lost. I even gave a speech to the Hopkins Women's Republican Club. I knew my material cold but did not have an obligatory opening joke until I noticed that the audience laughed each time the previous speaker mentioned President Truman. It was W. C. Fields's theory of irrational humor in action: every audience finds something funny for no apparent reason. So all I had to do was quickly construct a joke (regardless of quality) that ended with "Harry S. Truman." I got my laugh, and thus began my career as a speechwriter.

I acquired from Mac a moderate's feel for Republican politics that he had acquired from his father, who had managed eleven state campaigns in Minnesota and was rewarded by being named postmaster of St. Paul. I once asked Charley Moos why he never ran for elective office. "Yes, I thought about running for mayor," he replied. "I was pretty well known in that my name had been on every post box in the city for thirteen years. But whenever I got the urge, I'd read the telephone directory. You know, I only knew 5,000 people, and I concluded that even if all of them voted for me I'd still lose."

Like his father, Mac was a great storyteller. He liked to tell of the time in the 1940 presidential campaign when he and Hubert Humphrey, young instructors at the University of Minnesota, agreed to a thirty-minute debate on the campus radio station. They flipped a coin to see who would speak first. Humphrey won and spoke for twenty-seven minutes. "After that catastrophe at the hands of a demolition expert, I sought

From NET *(National Educational Television)*
NEWS, *1960, filming* Hats in the Ring *in New*
York. Malcolm Moos and (at far right) "Stephen
Hess, who wrote the series with Mr. Moos."

Malcolm Moos

refuge in the calm waters of academic life for the next eighteen years." That's the way Mac spoke. He once complimented my new suit as "a mighty fine pile of threads." Moving back and forth between academics and politics as he did, he was derided by some politicans as an egghead. Mac reminded them that the *Joy of Cooking* instructs, "Treat eggs gently. They like this consideration and will respond." Mac was to become president of the University of Minnesota in 1967. He was sixty-five when he died in 1982. Years later I gave a lecture at the university in the shadow of Moos Tower.

As soon as I got my bachelor's degree, in 1953, I was appointed a "junior instructor of political science," leading a section of Mac's American government course. Mac told me it was time to choose a career path. The appropriate question for a young man at the starting gate, as Harry McPherson asked in his wonderful book, *A Political Education,* should be, "What do you *want?*" I told Mac that academia was not the life I wanted. If not a scholar, a career in journalism? I was having fun writing freelance articles about Maryland politics for the *Christian Science Monitor* and the *New Leader,* a magazine whose orientation was liberal and anti-communist. I presented myself at the *Baltimore Evening Sun* to ask for a reporting job and was rejected. Well, then, if not the university or the press (as the media was then called), how about the law? Yet as my first class loomed, I could not see excitement in torts, and never walked up the front steps.

Mac then called his friend Bernard Lamb, the field director of the National Republican Campaign Committee in Washington, who hired me as his assistant. Barney had been mayor of Ho-Ho-Kus, and I enjoyed listening to his tales of New Jersey politics. My job was largely running groups of volunteers and computing simple targets for candidates. I learned never to give volunteers work that I was responsible for without carefully double-checking the results. I also met President Eisenhower's chief of staff, Sherman Adams, who was said to be the most powerful man in Washington. Once while I was serving him a canapé at a party Barney gave in his lovely garden on Capitol Hill, Adams asked, "Did you have any fun today?" Quite a nice question, I thought. "No," I replied, "I spent the day shopping for the food for this party."

Drafted

Nineteen fifty-six was the year Eisenhower was reelected and I was drafted into the army. At the Fort Dix Induction Center in New Jersey, a personnel specialist had to assign a number for me from the *Directory of Occupational Titles*. The more I tried to explain what I did, the more confused he looked. The *Directory* supposedly had a code for everything from beekeeper to striptease artist, but it apparently had no number for my occupation: politician.

In basic training at Fort Hood, I learned that I was short when I and my fellow draftees were lined up by height. In retrospect, I found this revealing, because I had never thought about it before. I also qualified on the carbine despite my ungenerous buddies saying that the graders simply wanted me to move along because I was taking too much time. In Germany my unit was placed in the Fulda Gap, the east-west route by which Soviet tanks would cross the Rhine; then suddenly I was told to report to Civil Affairs, 3rd Armored Division headquarters, on the outskirts of Frankfurt.

The office consisted of a colonel, a sergeant, and six privates. The work consisted of accounting for our tanks running over the Germans' cows, issuing invitations to the general's cocktail parties, and planning escape routes. The colonel I saluted was pudgy and about my height.

Colonel: "It's good to have a Foreign Service Officer with us, Hess."

"No, sir," I said. "I'm not a Foreign Service Officer." (So that's the occupation the confused personnel person at Fort Dix had assigned me!)

"Can you drive a truck?" the colonel asked, referring to the two-and-a-half-ton cargo truck known as a deuce-and-a-half.

"No, sir."

"Can you type?" he asked.

"No, sir."

Unable to meet either of the colonel's immediate needs, he sent me off to the beautiful Bavarian Alps for six weeks to attend a school for personnel specialists because it included a typing class. Do not graduate too high, my colonel instructed me, or the personnel section will grab you.

One night I visited the United States Information Service library in Frankfurt looking for a book about the Civil War and happened upon *The Biographical Directory of the United States Congress*, a tome weighing seven pounds and listing every legislator since the Continental Congress of 1774. As I skimmed names, some kept reappearing, over and over. Muhlenberg, Muhlenberg, Muhlenberg, Muhlenberg. Bayard, Bayard, Bayard, Bayard. Stocktons and Frelinghuysens. I knew of presidents named Adams, Harrison, and Roosevelt. But who were these same-name senators and congressmen? This was a fascinating slice of American history that I had not been taught in school. When not on guard duty, I spent my evenings compiling genealogies—some 300 of them. Perhaps they might be useful someday. A decade later, when the first volume of *America's Political Dynasties* was published in 1966, I wrote a letter of thanks to the USIS for providing the library that made the book possible. I received back a form explaining the procedure for recommending books for purchase.

Years later, after the military draft was replaced by the volunteer army, I published an essay addressed to my teenage sons about my two years in the military:

> The middle class draftee learns to appreciate a lot of talents (and the people who have them) that are not part of the lives you have known. . . . This will come from being thrown together with— and having to depend on—people who are very different from you and your friends. Moreover, if you can't fix a jeep or dig a hole in the frozen ground, these other people are a lot more valuable than you are. It is no small lesson to recognize their worth. And it is equally useful to learn to fit together with them in a community. For you, too, have skills that are valuable to them.

The Eisenhower White House, 1958–61

After my four months on the Republican National Committee payroll, in January 1959 I became a special assistant in the White House Office.

When Fred Greenstein of Princeton was interviewing Sherman Adams for his seminal 1982 book, *The Hidden Hand Presidency,* he asked President Eisenhower's first chief of staff to evaluate the cabinet members—Secretary of State John Foster Dulles, Secretary of Defense Charles Wilson, Secretary of the Treasury George Humphrey, Secretary of Agriculture Ezra Taft Benson—then White House staff such as Press Secretary James Hagerty and Staff Secretary Andrew Goodpaster, national security advisers, economic advisers, and others. Finally, Greenstein asked, "What about Steve Hess?" To which the acerbic Adams replied, "Now you're really scraping the barrel!" (This is my wife's favorite story.)

"To be young was very heaven," wrote Wordsworth, and I was young, gainfully employed by the president of the United States, and with my very own personal, private office: Room 276, in the Executive Office Building across from the White House. There was also a connecting office for my very own secretary.

What a building! This monstrous example of General Grant Renaissance, built between 1871 and 1888, once housed the entire State Department, War Department, and Navy Department. It was a building so odd of construction that should one step give way, five floors of steps would come tumbling down. The huge flower pots outside the main entrance were designed by Captain Douglas MacArthur when he was superintendent of the building. Young Theodore Roosevelt and Franklin Roosevelt had offices there when they served as assistant secretary of the navy. I loved this presence of the past. My brass doorknobs were emblazoned with the seal of the War Department; the long iron pipes fastened high on my walls once held the regimental banners of defeated armies. I had a conference table capable of seating ten, and at meetings I made sure a White House notepad lay at each place so that my guests could "steal" them. Then too, I loved this building because it was just so ugly.

The story goes that President Coolidge was given a tour and asked only one question: "Is it insured against fire and earthquake?" "Of course, Mr. President." To which Coolidge replied, "What a pity." (Unfortunately for the tale's veracity, government buildings are not insured.)

The view from what Sherman Adams considered my barrel was spectacular. Angling across a gated street to the West Wing of the White House, it allowed me to watch important people avoid the press by entering through a side door, or watch helicopters land on the orange stripes that had been placed on the South Lawn—the president holding tight to his fedora as he disembarked under the windy whirl of the chopper's blades—or watch the red-and-white candy-striped canopies sheltering Mrs. Eisenhower's lawn parties.

Daily I walked from one end of the White House to get to Mac's office in the East Wing. I entered the West Wing on the ground floor and took a little elevator to the first floor. This took a minute or two, and on one trip I was alone with the secretary of state, Christian Herter, back from an important Geneva conference. What to say? "Did you have a good trip, Mr. Secretary?" His reply was yes. I continued traveling along an outdoor colonnade. If the weather was good, Ike might be driving golf balls on the South Lawn, wearing a tan sweater and cap. I asked a Secret Service man for some instruction: He told me the president was practicing with a nine iron, used to lift a shot over an obstacle and stop dead. I estimated he was hitting the ball eighty or ninety yards. To this nongolfer he seemed to have a nice, effortless swing. If the weather was bad, I detoured through the residence, sometimes tripping over toys left by the grandchildren (tourists were on the floor above). On the outside, I passed Mamie's rose garden and, if the First Family had been watching a movie last night, stacked cans of film. I was fascinated by Ike's viewing habits. Stealing a peek at the film's label, I noticed he had been watching *Gunfighters of Abilene.* He loved Westerns. I was told that the projectionist's log would show that Ike saw over 200 Westerns during his eight years in the White House. Jim Hagerty told me that Ike's favorite movie was *Angels in the Outfield,* a 1951 comedy about a short-tempered Pittsburgh Pirates manager who mended his ways in return for a little divine assistance on the ball field. Pete Aurand, the naval aide, told me that the president and British prime minister Harold Macmillan had spent an evening at Camp David watching *The Mouse That Roared,* the story of a tiny country that declares war on the United States, figuring that the loss would bring American aid and solve its economic problems. The choice must have had special meaning for Ike since he had already seen the movie. Under the arcade by the Rose Garden was the entrance to the White House swimming pool, not Ike's sport. There was a gymnasium of sorts, containing a punching bag, barbells, and an electric exercising bicycle, hardly up to downtown hotel standards. We could use the facilities at will except between 9 and 11 a.m., when it was reserved for wives. Swimming all by myself in a big pool didn't appeal to me, especially since the pool's temperature was 90 degrees.

Staff meetings took place in the Fish Room, across from the president's office. It was called the Fish Room because FDR kept his aquarium there. (It is now called the Roosevelt Room.) Every other week there was a required early morning briefing by the Central Intelligence Agency. The briefer always started with a joke. The best one I remember is this: "An Australian gets a new boomerang for Christmas and goes crazy trying to throw the old one away." This supposedly had something to do with the difficulties Communists had changing the party line. The briefer's worst joke: "A psychiatrist sits on a bus next to a young man who keeps pinching her. She is getting really annoyed. But then she asks herself, 'Why am I angry? After all, it's his problem.'" I can't remember what national security issue this was supposed to illustrate. I learned no secrets that I would not have known from a careful reading of the *New York Times.* And I would have had a few more hours of sleep.

On Wednesdays when the president was going to have a press conference we again trooped into the Fish Room at 8:30 a.m., this time to discuss questions that might be asked two hours later. Hagerty would distribute an outline of what he expected from the reporters. We were his backup, yet his predictions were rarely off by more than a question or two. Hagerty always knew which reporters to call on when he wanted to change the subject. Sarah McClendon, who ran a one-woman regional news service, was good for a question about some Texas concern regardless of the day's international crisis. Since presidential press conferences at that time were not broadcast live on radio or television, at noon a recording of the press conference was played in the White House Mess and we could check Hagerty's batting average.

Of our other staff meetings in the Fish Room, the most interesting were reports on overseas trips for those of us who stayed home, filled with odds and ends that we would not have read in the press, such as when the president brought a transistor clock-radio as a personal gift for the Queen of England and the thing would not work at the presentation at Balmoral Castle. Prince Philip was very polite, saying radio reception was always bad there. But Ike's gift would not even bring in static; another clock was flown from Washington in thirty-six hours. Or when Ann Whitman, the president's personal secretary, was assigned the room at Chequers in which Lady Jane Grey had been kept prisoner for two years and found that the room had a secret exit. Or when Walter Tkach, the assistant physician to the president, accompanied the vice president to Moscow and narrated the movies he took of Nixon and Khrushchev inside the Kremlin. The doctor was an okay photographer but could have used a good film editor. Or when Karl Harr, of the national security staff, reported on his trip to inspect the U.S. base at the South Pole.

Working at the White House was certainly different from what my life would have been in graduate school! There was a trip on the president's helicopter, whose interior was about as posh as a commercial airliner and sported the same innocuous beiges. We were going to see where my office would be inside a West Virginia mountain if the White House came under attack. It was the first time I had ever flown in a helicopter. I learned that helicopters are plenty noisy. They vibrate. Even the president's. I also remember worrying whether I would leave my family if such an attack actually happened.

There were also invitations to White House musicales and state dinners, tickets to the Army-Navy game in Philadelphia and the Westminster Dog Show, a viewing of the Fourth of July fireworks from the South Lawn. I bought a formal evening suit of white tie and tailcoat for $37 at a going-out-of-business sale. The suit was so heavy that to put it on was to feel encased. There were so few of us that even I was included at Chairman Khrushchev's White House reception—we in tails, the Russians in black business suits. The entertainment was Fred Waring and His Pennsylvanians offering "Zip-a-Dee-Doo-Dah," "Battle Hymn of the Republic," and "Dem Dry Bones." President Eisenhower, in his memoirs, wrote that Khrushchev "seemed to enjoy thoroughly" the "robust" music. The audience was small, perhaps 150 in all. I was seated close to the Russians, and my notes record they "sat in stony silence."

The Staff

On September 22, 1958, Sherman Adams gave a dramatic, eight-minute national speech on radio and TV resigning as President Eisenhower's chief of staff. It was almost the same day as my "first words" as a presidential speechwriter. Adams was replaced by retired Major General Wilton (Jerry) Persons as the assistant to the president, the chief of staff's actual title. Until the end of the administration, a little over two years later, I served in a White House run by Jerry Persons, whose reign is now hardly noted by historians. A well-regarded study of the office, *The Gatekeepers*, by Chris Whipple, does not even mention Persons's name (though Whipple rightly notes Adams's heavy-handed management style). Adams and Persons were of opposite temperament and management style—Adams the flinty, all-business New Englander, Persons the charming, humorous southerner. Although he had an MBA from Harvard Business School, Persons was chosen to be a conciliator and was therefore not overly concerned with running a taut ship. He allowed more staff direct access to the president and was less interested in scrutinizing what went before his boss. Yet the change from Adams to Persons did not notably affect the operations of the government. After six years, staff members were proficient in their assignments, comfortable in their relations with each other, and now part of a waning administration. As a newcomer to the administration, however, I have always been grateful to

General Persons for this wonderful work environment in a place that has not always been known as a wonderful work environment.

Because our White House was so compartmentalized, and we were so intent on not minding the business of our colleagues, the mess during the Eisenhower years may have played a more important role in creating an atmosphere of collegiality than in other administrations. After the Adams-Goldfine imbroglio, matchbook covers reading "White House Mess" were reprinted with "White House Staff Mess." Located on the ground floor in the West Wing and run by the U.S. Navy, with the appropriate decor of ship's chest, nautical clock, and seascapes, and with our name-engraved napkin rings waiting for us, the mess offered food that was more than adequate and inexpensive. Almost every day I sat at the staff table, where that day's companions might be Assistant Staff Secretary John Eisenhower, the president's son and a talented man who I imagined would otherwise have been a wonderful college history professor; Staff Secretary Andrew Goodpaster, the quiet strategist who would someday head NATO; Bryce Harlow, who would influence my life in important ways; science adviser George Kistiakowsky, the Harvard chemist who once invented an edible explosive that Chinese guerrillas could smuggle through Japanese checkpoints; and Robert Montgomery, the movie actor of *Night Must Fall* fame, who would arrive at the White House to "direct" the president when Eisenhower gave televised speeches. They did not talk business, or even much "current events." Sometimes they told good stories, usually about former presidents—of whom their favorite was Calvin Coolidge. "He had a handshake like a cold fish." . . . "Mrs. Coolidge called him 'poppa.'" . . . "Mr. President, these young men are honored to have the privilege of drilling for you. Would you care to say a few words to them?" "No," said President Coolidge. I was a good listener and wrote down the stories when I got back to my office. On rare occasions I reserved my own table so that I could show off for an army buddy or a college classmate.

The staff had at least one "star," Captain Edward L. Beach, who had been the White House's naval aide from 1953 to 1957. Beach was also the author of the best-seller *Run Silent, Run Deep*. On May 10, 1960, I watched a helicopter return Ned Beach to the White House, where he was reporting to the president that he had taken the nuclear submarine the USS *Triton* on the first submerged voyage around the world in eighty-four days. The staff also had one "character"—Tom Stephens, the president's Irish-born appointments secretary. Stephens once wore one brown shoe and one black shoe to test whether the well-dressed president would notice (he didn't) and tried to organize a White House cricket team. It's a wonderful sport, he said, if you have a hangover.

What characterized the Eisenhower operation was its very small size. At the time, the staff mess might have seated about three dozen diners. Being able to lunch with my elders was a special advantage for me. When I returned to the White House in 1969, for example, this was not possible for young staffers. (In the Nixon White House, there were two seatings, separated by rank, and when I left Nixon in 1972, the White House had two dining rooms, again separated by rank.) Moreover, a remarkable number of my colleagues in Ike's sixth year had been there since the beginning. Twelve would serve the full two terms. This was not the two-year churn, where the White House may be most valued as a springboard to something more lucrative in the upper reaches of law, business, or the media. John Bragdon, the special assistant for public works planning, had even been Ike's classmate at West Point. Many staffers came to the White House as already functioning professionals. Press Secretary Jim Hagerty had been a professional press secretary, having served Tom Dewey in his two presidential campaigns; Jerry Persons ran congressional relations at the White House, as he had at the Pentagon during World War II, until he replaced Sherman Adams and turned the congressional relations portfolio over to Bryce Harlow, who had been his assistant at the Pentagon; lawyers came from Congress, not Wall Street. All this helped to explain the efficiency of Ike's operation.

There were also structural changes from the Truman presidency that have since become standard features of all White House staffs, including the positions of chief of staff, assistant for national security affairs, cabinet secretary, and staff secretary, and a greatly upgraded office of congressional relations. Collectively, these changes were designed to make sure that nothing fell through the cracks. Ike cared deeply about the importance of process. He tried to explain this to President-elect John F. Kennedy when they met after the 1960 election. He was not successful. "Organization cannot make a genius out of an incompetent," he said. "On the other hand, disorganization can scarcely fail to result in inefficiency."

The Eisenhower people were older than the Kennedy people (or even the Nixon people). They included retired CEOs of major corporations such as General Foods and Hart Schaffner & Marx. Could my youth have been helpful in my being so comfortably accepted? Perhaps I was nephew-like to some. Jerry Persons, a gentle general, seemed to find excuses to send me encouraging notes. My favorite friend was Clarence Randall, the president's assistant on foreign economic policy, who had been president of the Inland Steel Company when President Truman in 1952 ordered the secretary of commerce to seize the steel industry to block a threatened strike during the Korean War. Randall's defense of the steel industry was heard on radio and TV by an estimated 50 million people and turned him into an instant celebrity. (Randall and the steel industry challenged Truman's powers in court, and the Supreme Court took their side.) This was his greatest moment, and he wanted to tell me, as he had not written in his memoirs, that he had one regret: It had been inappropriate of him to attack *Mister* Truman rather than *President* Truman. The faux pas was still on his mind eight years later. Another of my ancient colleagues, Earle Chesney of the congressional relations staff, who had been assistant usher in the White House during the Hoover administration, drew a large cartoon portrait of me as a gift. It was not very good, but it was a kind gesture.

Unlike the Kennedy staff, which was heavy on professors, Ike's academics were more likely to be university presidents, notably James Killian of MIT, Gordon Gray of the University of North Carolina, Arthur Flemming of Ohio Wesleyan, and, of course, the president's brother, Milton Eisenhower, of Johns Hopkins. I counted six, including Harold Stassen of the University of Pennsylvania, who had twice been a leading candidate for the Republican Party's presidential nomination.

Adding up the retired CEOs and university presidents, I was struck by the number of my colleagues who had "stepped down" to serve as presidential assistants. Financially, at least, working at the White House was not the best job they had ever had. From A (Adams, Sherman) to Y (Young, Philip)—each with a brief biography and photograph—it is all in a sort of class yearbook, *White House Staff Book, 1953–61*, that I think is unique to the Eisenhower staff. My copy is number fifty-two. I have attached to the cover the following note: "To My Heirs: This is my most *valuable* book!"

Other than myself, there was only one person in his twenties. Phil Areeda was twenty-eight. But even then it was hard to think of Phil as young. The instant Ike left office in 1961, Phil became a professor of law at Harvard. In my diary I wrote, "In 25 years he will be a legend in Cambridge." When he died in 1995, at the age of sixty-five, his obituary in the *New York Times* quoted Supreme Court justice Stephen Breyer as once having said that "most lawyers would rather have the support of 'two paragraphs of Areeda on antitrust than four court of appeals and three Supreme Court Justices.'"

We were overwhelmingly male and white. Of the eighty-one of us who had mess privileges during Ike's eight years (excluding military officers), there were only three women and one African American on the senior staff. The women were Mary Jane McCaffree, personal secretary to the First Lady; Ann C. Whitman, secretary to the president; and Anne Wheaton, associate press secretary. The African American was E. Frederic Morrow, the administrative officer for special projects, a job that had more responsibility than the name suggests. The press proclaimed that Fred was "the first Negro Presidential aide in history." He penned a sad commentary on his former colleagues in his diary after overhearing a racist joke (later recounted in his book, *Black Man in the White House*): "I'm not going out of my way to look for incidents, and will not begin to wear my feelings on my sleeve, but I am determined that in the future I will speak out boldly and unequivocally in situations where persons are so crude as to forget that I am a human being before I am a Negro."

The moment that drove home to me this deep racial divide on the staff came at an event that should have been one of the happiest of my time there. My wife and I were invited to the state dinner on September 27, 1960, for Crown Prince Akihito and Princess Michiko of Japan. I think this rare honor came because I was, at twenty-six, the same age as the prince. The entertainment was billed as "An Evening with Gershwin" and included excerpts from *Porgy and Bess*. The role of Porgy was sung by Todd Duncan, the original Porgy; Bess was the great lyric soprano Camilla Williams, the first African American to perform regularly with a major American opera company. On arrival, we were given the names of our dinner partners: Camilla Williams and Todd Duncan. We were thrilled! Then I was taken to the side, where the White House social secretary whispered in my ear, apologizing for pairing us with the black entertainers.

The 1960 Election

In late spring of 1960, Jerry Persons directed me to write a detailed paper on the achievements of Ike's two terms to help guide the work of the Republican Platform Committee for the 1960 campaign. When the Platform Committee needed information, I would be its link to the White House. Platform drafting belongs to the party's convention and its nominee, not the president, but we were worried that there might be some drift away from Ike's accomplishments. I was there to offer guidance.

The Platform Committee's chairman was Charles Percy, the president of Bell & Howell, a creative business executive but a novice in politics. He did not like the convention's traditional parade of delegates reading platform planks. Instead, he wanted a film of what would be in the platform—a film that Percy himself would narrate. I was sent to a screening room in a New York City loft to help the filmmakers choose footage. The problem, of course, was that there was not yet a platform. So my job was to tell them what subjects the platform would most likely include. There would be a section on agriculture, so it would need farms and cows. It was a pretty standard assignment, but the filmmakers were not

DINNER

Pate de Foie Gras in Aspic
Chippers

Dry Sack   Horseradish Soup
Melba Toast
Celery Hearts
Queen and Ripe Olives

Chateau Coutet
a Barsac   Broiled Filet of Sole Amandine
1937   Danish Tomatoes
Boston Brown Bread

Beaune   Roast Saddle of Lamb
Greves   Crabapple Garnish
1952   Fresh Mint Sauce
Brown Potato Balls
French String Beans
Bread Sticks

Bibb Lettuce in Salad
Green Goddess Dressing
Pol Roger   Cheese Straws
1952

Frozen Rum Pudding
Butterscotch Sauce
Lady Fingers
Salted Nuts

Candies

Demitasse

THE WHITE HOUSE
Tuesday, September 27, 1960

politicians. Yet this did produce one unusual moment. For the segment on national defense, we discovered that the building's elevator operator was a Russian, and for $10 we had him record a missile countdown in Russian: *Desiat . . . deviat . . . vosem . . . pusk!*"

The Platform Committee met at Chicago's Sheraton-Blackstone Hotel a week before the delegates were to arrive in the city. On July 22, we gathered in Percy's suite to await the last of eight subcommittee reports. Eight secretaries were standing by to cut stencils of the draft platform so that the full committee could begin its final deliberations at 9 a.m. the next morning. But the real work of platform-drafting was over, or so thought those of us with the chairman. At 10:30 the phone rang— and it was obvious from Percy's response that this was no ordinary call. Nixon, it turned out, had secretly flown to New York to meet with New York governor Nelson Rockefeller in the governor's Fifth Avenue apartment. Their supporters represented the two wings of the Republican Party, and this was apparently Nixon's gambit to unite them behind his nomination. Now they were calling to tell Percy what they wanted put into the platform. There were three phones in the suite—Percy was on one, Rod Perkins, Rockefeller's representative, was on the second, and I was one of several rotating on the third. The call lasted nearly four hours, except for fifteen minutes at midnight when the hotel's switchboard operator pulled the plug and went home. This resulted in the so-called Compact of Fifth Avenue.

The Platform Committee's reaction was explosive: Barry Goldwater, the conservative leader, called it "Nixon's surrender, the Munich of the Republican party." Actually, there weren't that many changes from the original committee draft, but Nixon failed to perceive the symbolic aspects—his having gone to Rockefeller, rather than Rockefeller having gone to him; the Compact having been released by Rockefeller, not Nixon; and the opening words, "The Vice-President and I met today at my home in New York City. The meeting took place at the Vice-President's request." The Platform Committee's revolt lasted thirty-six hours. "We will not be dictated to by Rockefeller!" The inexperienced Percy moved aside to work on his film narration, and Vice Chairman

Mel Laird, the time-tested congressman from Wisconsin, took over. Nixon rushed to Chicago to calm the delegates.

While the dust was settling, I found I had a unique problem: in all the confusion, the words praising the United States Information Agency had been deleted from the platform. That meant we were left with a film to cover content and, in this case, no content to be covered. Perhaps this was not a big deal, but it was to me since I had been the go-between on what was in the film. I rushed to see Kentucky senator John Sherman Cooper, the foreign policy chairman. Was there any way to get his committee to put back those few lines in praise of the USIA? With the clock ticking, Senator Cooper got the language reinstated, a feat I considered magical, in light of how overheated the delegates now were about every word. I later thanked Senator Cooper by writing a speech for him.

The next unexpected problem arrived on August 24, when the president held his weekly Wednesday morning press conference. The press conference started at 10:30 and, on the president's instructions, was to end promptly a half hour later. It included an exchange that would reverberate throughout the campaign:

> Charles H. Mohr (*Time* magazine): Many people have been trying to get at the degree that he [Nixon] has—I don't want to use the word "participated"—but acted in important decisions, and it is hard to pin down.
>
> President Eisenhower: Well, it seems to me that there is some confusion here—haziness—that possibly needs a lot of clarification. . . . So the Vice President has participated for eight years, or seven-and-a-half years, in all of the consultative meetings that have been held. . . . But no one, and no matter how many differences or whether they are all unanimous—no one has the decisive power. There is no voting.
>
> Mohr: We understand that the power of decision is entirely yours, Mr. President. I just wondered if you could give us an example of a major idea of his that you adopted in that role, as the decider and final—

Eisenhower: If you give me a week, I might think of one. I don't remember.

Jack Bell, the senior wire service reporter, hurriedly closed the news conference: "Thank you, Mr. President."

The staff gathered for lunch in the mess at noon to listen to a recording of what our boss had just said, but I cannot recall our comments. Probably we were respectfully silent. I know I was stunned, and the next day I asked John Eisenhower if he could throw any light on his father's "give me a week" remark. John's explanation was that the president was anxious to conclude the press conference and what he meant was "I will be back next week and then will answer your question." This last-question-out-the-door defense was a plausible enough explanation for Ike's misstatement; he was famous for answers that left reporters confused. (Some were delivered for that very purpose.) But neither Ike nor the reporters returned to the question at next Wednesday's news conference.

Years later John and I returned to the question of his father and Nixon. "I never regarded it as much of a secret that Bob Anderson would have been Dad's first choice as his successor, had Dad possessed the power to appoint," he wrote me, referring to Robert B. Anderson, Ike's treasury secretary from 1957 to 1961. "Perhaps the reason I found it no secret is that I heard Dad say it so often. But without a doubt Nixon was Dad's first choice among those whom he considered had a prayer of being elected."

I think of Ike's "give me a week" comment as the most devastating blow to Nixon's campaign. In an instant, Eisenhower had severed Nixon's position as the candidate of experience. In the first Kennedy-Nixon debate in September, reporter Sander Vanocur asked for clarification of Ike's remark, and Nixon worked hard to give an answer (or multiple answers):

Well, I would suggest, Mr. Vanocur, that if you know the president, that that was probably a facetious remark. . . . I think it would be improper for the president of the United States to disclose the instances in which members of his official family had made recommendations. . . . I do not say that I have made decisions, and would say that no president should ever allow anybody else to make the major decisions. . . . I can only say that my experience is there for the people to consider. Senator Kennedy is there for people to consider.

The simple answer was that the president had made a mean and thoughtless comment about the man who had been his loyal vice president for eight years and was now his party's nominee for president.

On August 19, three weeks after the convention in Chicago, General Persons called us together to discuss the role of the White House staff in the campaign. It was going to be modest. Bob Merriam, who had once run for mayor of Chicago, was going to be our liaison to the campaign, and I was tasked with representing the White House at the daily Answer Desk meetings seeking responses to opposition attacks. According to my notes of the time, we were told that caution was to be used in talking with newspapermen, who would try to drive a wedge between the president and the vice president; that regular CIA briefings were to be canceled; and that White House form letters were being rewritten to make them more personal and to feature the vice president more prominently. Most important of all: "White House staff are requested to remain until January 20 unless there is an emergency." Persons's worry was that he still had an administration to run and that we were prematurely packing our bags.

Eisenhower's staff was not a group that would stay on in Washington as media celebrities or high-priced lobbyists. Their future was more about fishing and sailing. There were some successes: Brigadier General Andrew Goodpaster was awarded a fourth star and, in 1977, was summoned out of retirement to oversee the U.S. Military Academy at West Point in the wake of a cadet cheating scandal. But there was also tragedy: Colonel William G. Draper, who had been Eisenhower's personal pilot since Ike left Columbia University to command NATO, who flew

President Truman to his historic meeting with General MacArthur, who piloted General Albert C. Wedemeyer on his tour of China, and who once told me he had crossed oceans 232 times, not counting Hawaii and Bermuda, hanged himself after a heart attack that forced him to give up flying. Bill Draper was forty-four years old.

I was one of only four people on Eisenhower's staff who returned to the White House when, eight years later, Nixon finally won the presidency. The other three were Arthur Burns, Bryce Harlow, and Brad Patterson, who eventually would write several important books on White House operations.

Still, by mid-September, Mac Moos and I were preparing drafts for what we believed was to be Ike's active campaign around the country on behalf of Nixon and his running mate, U.S. ambassador to the UN Henry Cabot Lodge. Yet as the weeks went by, it was beginning to take on the overtones of Gilbert and Sullivan's *The Pirates of Penzance,* with the policemen singing "We go, we go," and the general responding "Yes, but you don't go." Why wasn't he going? The answer was that Mamie Eisenhower and Howard Snyder, the president's doctor, were deeply concerned about Ike's health and secretly asked Nixon to decline Ike's offer of a vigorous schedule. Ike, anxious to campaign, was confused and irritated by Nixon's turndown. That story would eventually reach the public in a biography of Nixon that I co-authored in 1968.

In the campaign's last week, the president finally spoke at rallies in Philadelphia, in and around New York City, and in Cleveland. On November 2, in Garden City, New York, he said this about Nixon and Lodge:

> For eight years I have worked intimately with the two men who are today your national candidates. I know them intimately. I have seen them undertake the tasks which I have requested of them, with the utmost enthusiasm, never with a complaint or with any excuses for avoiding a duty. Instead, no matter what it meant in sleepless nights and long roads of travel, they have always been ready to do it. And the point is, they have done it

effectively. They know. They know about the problems that are brought before the President.

White House reporters told me they had rarely seen Eisenhower speak with the passion of that week. Kennedy was elected with 49.71 percent of the total vote; Nixon received 49.55 percent. If 11,424 votes had shifted in five states, Nixon would have won. Nixon's campaign had errors for everyone. Everyone had a favorite "what if," and everyone was right. What if Eisenhower had not said "give me a week"? What if Eisenhower had made a few more speeches in the right places? Ike apparently agreed: "One of the biggest mistakes of my political career was not working harder for Dick Nixon in 1960."

Speeches

The White House East Wing, where Mac's office was located, also housed the First Lady's staff and the military aides, which were to provide a special gift in the guise of Ralph Williams, assistant naval aide to the president, who dropped in to ask Mac if he could be of help. Most of the military aides were West Point or Annapolis graduates. Ralph decidedly was not. When his boss was away and Commander Williams had to wear his uniform, it looked as if he had shrunk inside it. Ralph had an accounting degree from the University of Texas and was a reserve ensign in the Supply Corps. He had served at Pearl Harbor and Tarawa during World War II. Later he compiled a long record of winning the prestigious Naval Institute's annual essay contest. Mac, having never been in the military, was delighted to add an expert on national security to the team.

So our speechwriting team consisted of two full-time staffers and one part-timer. A lively memoir by David Litt, a speechwriter for President Barack Obama, counted eight people in 2011 on that presidential speechwriting team. They appear to have been very busy. He described their "personal space" as less "than Walmart during a Black Friday sale." My 1959 office, as already noted, had a conference table seating ten.

It was the blood oath of every Eisenhower speechwriter to avoid claims of credit. The words belonged to the president, period. But on the chance that time and historians might make a difference, here is a semihidden fact: Ralph Williams invented Ike's most famous line: "In the councils of government, we must guard against the acquisition of unwarranted influence, whether sought or unsought, by the military-industrial complex."

As Ralph remembered, "I got into writing the thing, [and] it looked like what we were really talking about was a military-industrial complex rather than war-based. I think the 'complex' part of it came—you know, you get to the end of a sentence and you don't know how to end it up and this word comes to you and you write it in and that's the way it fits and that's the way it came out."

I did not work on this great speech. When Mac and Ralph were doing the drafting, with major assistance from the president's brother, Milton, I was working on a related study of the growing number of retired military personnel who were entering careers in defense-related private industries.

After a Moos-Williams-Hess session to discuss an upcoming speech, we each drafted our ideas independently; then Mac, who called himself "the carpenter," would piece them together to present to the president. The three of us were a happy team. Compared to the output of more recent presidents, we were not overworked. I even found time to help a colleague or two with an occasional speech draft, which must have added to my popularity, and Mac, who had a busy speaking schedule of his own, was often in demand. A few years ago at a Gridiron Dinner, Paul Ward, White House correspondent for the *Baltimore Sun* during the Eisenhower years, told me that around the press room I was called "the ghost's ghost." It was news to me.

Among Mac's duties were protecting speech drafts from "important people"—and sometimes other staffers—who knew just what Eisenhower should be saying. Mac's predecessor, the law professor Arthur Larson, according to his biographer had felt the staff was trying to insulate him from the president and that "Eisenhower occasionally became exasperated enough to remind Larson whose speech it was they were working on." But Mac's low-key style was a comfortable fit with president and staff.

The president liked to start with a complete draft of a speech and would become more and more involved, draft after subsequent draft, until it took on his character. A major speech might go through ten drafts. (A draft only changed its number after it had been edited by the president. The Farewell Address was the result of a remarkable twenty-nine drafts.)

Because of Ike's famously awkward responses at press conferences, it always surprised my friends when I told them he was a superb editor and had once been a speechwriter for Douglas MacArthur. To prove my point, I showed them a draft of a fairly routine speech I kept in my desk: "Greetings from the President to the First National Urban County Congress, March 16, 1959 (To Be Delivered by the Vice President)." Yet despite the speech's relative unimportance, the draft was overloaded with Ike's soft-pencil corrections, his changes often an improvement on what I had written for him.

Because of the president's medical history—he had had a mild stroke in 1957—I tried to shorten sentences whenever I could, but he automatically returned to the way he had been taught. Occasionally he would employ a rhetorical flourish, which most often came from me since my concentration was the political stuff, such as calling the Republican Party a "hibernating elephant" after it badly lost a midterm election: "I deeply regret that some people look upon our party as a kind of hibernating elephant who wakes with a mighty trumpet blast at election time and then rests calmly until the next campaign." This phrase became the subject of a Herblock cartoon, with the caption "Be glad he's hibernating—there's been talk that he was dead."

Ike was essentially an informational speaker whose objective was to say something as clearly and precisely as possible. He did not have a signature style, unlike Nixon or Kennedy. I like to think of his nonstyle as

GREETINGS FROM THE PRESIDENT TO THE FIRST NATIONAL
URBAN COUNTY CONGRESS, MARCH 16, 1959 (TO BE DELIVERED
BY THE VICE PRESIDENT)

*It is a great privilege to send, through
my great friend, the Vice-President, warm*

I am especially pleased to greet the First National Urban

greetings to   To grapple with the growing problems

County Congress. In few areas do we so urgently need an assembly *urbanization*

for the careful analysis and the exchange of experiences and ideas.

As the elected and appointed representatives of the 300 urban

counties in which more than six out of every 10 Americans now

thousand

live, you are faced with a myriad of new challenges. Further, your

responsibility for the welfare of your fellow citizens will be greatly

increased as an estimated one million acres become urban and

I am told that

suburban each year. By 1975 urban areas will occupy twice the

present

areas now covered.

our history of ancient times tell us

The very origin of organized society was a direct result of *that cities and organized county began
and developed side by side. For a*

urbanization. In early times as the Middle East became arid people *number of reasons people tended to congregate
in groups along the*

gathered by the great rivers and springs. To insure a proper

To be obeyed by all

distribution of water, rules and regulations were set up and thus

society, ruled by law, was born. To enforce the law political power

was organized.

Indeed The word politics means the "affairs of the city".

Though later ages,

calm, straightforward, and sincere. I can remember only one joke that Ike told in a speech during our tenure. It was at the Football Hall of Fame Dinner in Canton, Ohio, on October 28, 1958:

> I am prompted to tell one story, not about football, but about a very great football player and coach when he was a very small boy. The hero—or villain—was Bo McMillin.
>
> Bo grew up in a small Texas town, where he had the reputation of being the best-behaved boy in the whole village. One Sunday morning the town constable, walking down the street, saw Bo standing in front of the village jewelry store, and strangely, he had a very large brick in his hand. He stood there at least ten minutes, and suddenly he threw that brick right through the plate glass window.
>
> Stunned, the constable asked Bo how a model boy could ever do such a thing.
>
> "Well, sir," said Bo, "you see I'm a Catholic—and today I'm on my way to confession. And my trouble is, sir, I was just a mite short of material."

This pathetic joke was contributed by Mac, who had a stockpile of good stories. Unfortunately, this was not one of them.

A worry for me—in the language and image department—was that I was two generations removed from the president. (He was born in 1890, making him forty years my senior.) Ike was most comfortable with colleagues who were within a ten-year radius (note the ages of his cabinet officers). My special concern was to choose words that he might have chosen. Sometimes I got it right—as in his March 16, 1959, radio and television speech, "Security in the Free World." In a section on concentrating "our resources on those things we need most," the president said, "The first model of any new piece of equipment is always relatively primitive. The first sewing machine, the first typewriter, the first automobile—all left much to be desired. And even the rockets that dazzle us today will soon become the Model T's—the Tin Lizzies—of the Missile Age."

An article in the *Washington Daily News* took note. "President Eisenhower tossed in a nostalgic term during his grim talk to the nation Monday night. . . . To most people under 40 years of age, the Model T is a well enough known name, but Tin Lizzie is something else, for it has not been a popular usage since 1925."

Breaking the White House rule on anonymity, I instantly sent the clipping to my mother in Philadelphia to boast of the author's identity. It was a mite-sized accomplishment. But not for me!

My special pride as a speechwriter, however, was to invent a word. It was Ike's last speech of the midterm election, delivered on October 31, 1958, and I was tired of calling the Democrats "the party of gloom and doom," as I had been told to do. So I invented "gloomdoggle." If a boondoggle is a maker of unnecessary work, often used in the 1930s to disparage the New Deal, then a gloomdoggle must be a maker of unnecessary gloom.

Late that afternoon the White House minders came to Mac's office in the East Wing to review our draft: They hated gloomdoggle! I could hardly withstand this force. But again I was lucky. Mac and family lived in Baltimore, and Mac's wife, Tracey, arrived for a dinner party. She was a notably ebullient person and fearlessly entered our debate—and she loved "gloomdoggle." The West Wing gentlemen let the word stand, probably thinking that Ike would veto it anyway. But Ike also loved "gloomdoggle."

On Friday night, four days before Election Day, the White House staff bus took us over to the Fifth Regiment Armory in Baltimore to cheer our leader. After the speech, hawkers were selling the bulldog edition of Saturday's *Baltimore Sun*. Ike's speech commanded a headline of eight columns, capital letters in the boldest type short of declaring war:

IKE CALLS DEMOCRATS 'GLOOMDOGGLERS' IN SPEECH HERE CLOSING THE CAMPAIGN

The story, written by the paper's chief political correspondent, began: "President Eisenhower, closing his personal campaign for election of a Republican Congress, last night called the Democrats 'gloomdogglers' who offer the voters 'both sides of every issue.'" I paid five cents for a paper, and Mr. Avery, the White House carpenter, made me a gift of the framed page. To this day, it is the only piece of political memorabilia in my office. The *New York Times*, in error, put a hyphen between "gloom" and "doggler" in its story. I wish I could say the word entered into popular usage, but to the best of my knowledge I am the only person, other than President Eisenhower, who has ever used "gloomdoggler" a second time.

For those tabulating winners and losers: The 1958 congressional elections were truly filled with "gloom and doom" for the Republicans. Democrats picked up thirteen seats in the Senate and forty-seven in the House of Representatives, greatly increasing the majorities they already enjoyed.

If ever there was divine intervention on behalf of a harried speechwriter, it came on January 17, 1960, when I was working on "Dinner with Ike." This was a big deal: eighty-three fundraising dinners across the country connected by closed-circuit TV, with Richard Nixon in Chicago, Nelson Rockefeller in Washington, Henry Cabot Lodge in Pittsburgh, and President Eisenhower accepting the tributes in Los Angeles.

The piece of paper in my typewriter was still blank.

Then in my in-box the following letter appeared:

My dear Mr. President,

   I have just turned 21 years of age. I am now old enough to vote and mature enough to take part in political elections. My problem is, which party am I best suited to serve? I thought you would be able to help me by telling me what the Republican Party stands for.

   What are its goals and in what way may I help it to achieve them?

   Shirley Jean Havens

   Arvada, Colorado

Here is the divine intervention part: I had nothing to do with presidential correspondence. The correspondence section at the White House had never before forwarded to me a letter addressed to the president, nor would it ever do so again.

Would the president, I asked, like to address his Los Angeles speech to Shirley Jean?

The president loved the idea. He picked up the phone and called Aksel Nielson, a Denver banker and good friend, and asked him to go to Arvada and report back to him on Shirley Jean. (Maybe she was a communist or something.) Nielson reported that Shirley Jean was polite, pretty, a mother of two, the wife of an apprentice plumber, and lived in a trailer. Equally attractive: she had written the same letter to Harry Truman and had received a gruff reply to go read a book. (Ike was also furious that Shirley Jean's letter had been kicking around the White House for several months unanswered.)

From the president's speech on January 27:

> Before leaving early in December for a tour of foreign nations, I received a letter from a young lady, who lives in Arvada, Colorado. . . . Since that time, the letter has been much on my mind, but I have had no opportunity to answer it properly. Thinking about this evening's dinner, I asked friends to invite her and her husband to the Denver dinner, in the hope that I may convince her that she wants to be a Republican. So—Shirley Jean, to you, and I trust, to all other young or undecided voters I can reach, here is my answer.

There is more to the story. After I wrote about Shirley Jean in a 2008 book, I got a letter from her daughter telling me about her late mother's life and the glory that radiated to her from the speech. "Up until that time her life had been quiet and sheltered," she wrote. "Because of the exposure she made many good friends over the years, and was active in Republican campaigns. She was a wonderful example to me of community involvement and commitment."

Finally, when the locale of the president's Farewell Address was changed from Congress to the Oval Office, where it could be broadcast on national television, Jerry Persons concluded that there was now room in the congressional schedule to create a sort of second farewell. My assignment was to draft a narrative of Eisenhower's eight-year presidency that could be read into the *Congressional Record* by the House clerk. "So don't worry about length," Persons said. My problem was how to put together a 6,500-word message in less than three weeks. Simple: just dust off the exercise on "President's Achievements" that I wrote in the spring for the Republican Platform Committee, update it, change tense. This exercise accounted for 71 percent of the Annual Message to the Congress on the State of the Union, on January 12, 1961.

Still, having to summarize the president's record on civil rights worried me. He had done some exemplary work in those areas where his constitutional powers were most obvious: this largely related to desegregation in the District of Columbia, ending discrimination in federal employment and contracting, and completing Truman's desegregation of the armed forces. But responding to *Brown v. Board of Education*, the decision that ended legal segregation in public schools, his statement looked modest compared to the need: "The Supreme Court has spoken and I am sworn to uphold the constitutional processes in this country; and I will."

Now, in this last opportunity as president to address civil rights, what would he want to tell the American people? My words for him went through three drafts of "light editing." Ike concluded: "This pioneering work in civil rights must go on. Not only because discrimination is morally wrong, but also because its impact is more than national—it is world-wide."

There is a moment of joy for presidential speechwriters when they have something to do with a statement of great importance—in truth, speechwriters will admit this is not often.

"Discrimination is morally wrong" was to be my moment.

Remembering Ike

He had "that rare and inexplicable power to make others trust him," John Rhodehamel wrote of George Washington. This also was Ike's gift. It was not a small talent to be a comforting president. The 1950s were dangerous years.

To commemorate the 125th anniversary of his birth, in 2015 Gettysburg College published a slim book, *Encounters with Eisenhower*, a collection of personal reminiscences, beginning with entries from late 1942 when Ike was in North Africa. Co-editor Michael Birkner urged me to contribute. I kept stalling. Every writer knows it is much more difficult to write a hundred words than a thousand. What brief story could add to what was important to me about Ike? On deadline, I wrote:

October 14, 1959: The White House

We presented the president with two gifts for his 69th birthday—a huge cake and a red maple tree for the White House lawn. Hurrying to the presentation ceremony, Fay Steiner, Ralph Williams's secretary, unexpectedly ran into the president.

"I'm late," she stammered.

"Well," replied the president, "they can't do anything until we arrive."

Others told similar stories. "1949: Germany, I was in a hurry and running like hell. . . . I just ran straight into Gen. Eisenhower and knocked him flat. . . . I was expecting all kinds of dire punishments, but Ike picked himself up, brushed the dust off his clothing, and said, 'Just an accident, soldier, just an accident,' and went on his way." My White House colleague Roemer McPhee's story in *Encounters with Eisenhower* told how Ike's cabinet meetings always started with a prayer; after leaving one session, he heard the president say, "Jesus Christ, I forgot the prayer!"

I do not wish to suggest some angelic quality to the man. His smile may have been gene-driven, but he had trained long and hard to assume command, and there must have been a certain artifice to what he felt

*Presidential doodle on the back of State of the Union
draft, January 10, 1961. Perhaps a self-portrait?*

necessary for leadership. Plenty of others, generals and presidents, never learned this lesson.

He was the most popular general of a just war and twice overwhelmingly elected president, a genial, shrewd, optimistic, confident product of small-town Middle America. Since he had spent so much time abroad, his presidency had a somewhat anomalous international cast despite the president's rather conventional beliefs. A newcomer to partisan politics, he expressed considerable irritation at the art of politics, yet understood the mood of the electorate. He spent his political capital only when it made a difference, avoided lost causes, let others take the blame for miscues, and retained the confidence of his constituency. Republican losses in the 1954 midterm election, for instance, were blamed on Agriculture Secretary Ezra Taft Benson, not Eisenhower. One poll had 33 percent of farmers giving Benson a poor rating, while only 8 percent considered Eisenhower's performance inadequate. It was as if the president and the secretary of agriculture worked for different administrations. Ike's political genius was that he was able to successfully present himself as the anti-politician.

His aspirations as president had two overriding objectives: peace abroad and a balanced budget at home. He left a legacy of peace, and, we now find, eight years is a long time for us to be peaceful. At home, his most important achievement was the creation of a 41,000-mile Interstate Highway System, though he left a backlog of other needs for subsequent presidents to sort out, with successes and failures.

For Ike, it all came together in his Farewell Address. Ralph Williams's memorable contribution, "the military-industrial complex," was there to illustrate the speech's central, basic theme:

> Whether foreign or domestic, great or small, there is a recurring temptation to feel that some spectacular and costly action could become the miraculous solution to all current difficulties. . . . But each proposal must be weighed in light of a broader consideration: the need to maintain balance in and among national programs— balance between the private and the public economy, balance between cost and hoped for advantage—balance between the clearly necessary and the comfortably desirable; balance between our essential requirements as a nation and the duties imposed by the nation upon the individual; balance between actions of the moment and the national welfare of the future. Good judgment seeks balance and progress; lack of it eventually finds imbalance and frustration.

This was quintessential Eisenhower—balance. Every year on Ike's birthday, October 14, there should be room for a joint session of Congress to remember his parting words.

The year after Eisenhower's retirement, 1962, the Harvard professor Arthur M. Schlesinger Sr. asked a blue-ribbon panel of seventy-five experts, mostly academic historians, to grade the presidents of the United States. The results placed Eisenhower in a tie with Chester Arthur, one notch above Andrew Johnson, at the very bottom of the "average" category. Years passed: archives opened, new historians arrived, old historians reconsidered. Professor Arthur M. Schlesinger Jr., following his father, conducted the poll again in 1996: Eisenhower had risen to the "near great" category.

The evening before Ike was driven from Washington to Gettysburg, Pennsylvania, where he would live in retirement until his death in 1969, I wrote this note of thanks and appreciation:

Dear Mr. President:

I shall leave your administration at noon, January 20, with deep sadness. You have given me the rare opportunity to serve under an inspired leader. You have given me the opportunity to serve with fine and dedicated colleagues. You have given me the opportunity to try to be of service to our country. To you, sir, I am eternally grateful.

I add my humble wish for the future good health and happiness of you and Mrs. Eisenhower.

Respectfully yours,
Stephen Hess

Nixon

Interregnum, 1961

Now I had to find new employment.

Among my White House colleagues, I first sought the wisdom of my favorite elder, Clarence Randall, the steel magnate. "Go out and make money," he told me. "Then come back into government." This matter-of-fact suggestion implied (to him at least) that it would not be difficult. It was sound advice even if it did not appeal to me.

Next, the incoming Kennedy administration offered me a job as communications director for the secretary of labor. I was surprised and flattered. It might have been fine for Douglas Dillon, Eisenhower's deputy secretary of state, to become Kennedy's treasury secretary (although it infuriated Ike), but a young person does not advance himself by switching parties. I declined with thanks.

Why not a job with a senator, then? My friend Steve Horn had come to Washington from Stanford on a legislative fellowship. He then wanted some executive experience before returning to teaching, so I arranged for him to meet Jim Mitchell, Ike's labor secretary, who hired him. Now Steve was trying to return the favor by connecting me with Senator Thomas Kuchel of California. Wasn't Hess-to-Horn/Horn-to-Hess the way Washington works!

Tom Kuchel was a nice man and my type of moderate Republican. He promised that together, we would explore grand topics. What I did not know was how politically vulnerable he was, wedged between the rival factions of Richard Nixon and Senator William Knowland, who represented shades of conservatism. As a result, he chose to play the "home card," and for the six weeks I was with him in January and February 1961, I wrote speech after speech in praise of or in defense of every product, produce, or plant in the state of California. It was painful. I felt trapped.

Perhaps I had been spoiled by having just been a presidential speech-writer, part of a group that feels itself more exalted than other political scribblers and even has its own society, named for Judson Welliver, an obscure assistant to Warren G. Harding, who was said to have been the first professional to hold this job on a White House staff. The political heirs of Judson Welliver meet for dinner every other year, now at the home of Chris Matthews (speechwriter for Jimmy Carter), and give short, wistfully funny speeches to each other about the foibles of our former bosses. What we do not say is how much of our writing is what we call "Rose Garden rubbish." Still, our leaden efforts ended up in ersatz leather volumes, *The Public Papers of the Presidents*, each year's tome weighing about four pounds.

Moreover, I would learn that in Washington, political workers tend to be a better fit when employed under Article I or Article II of the Constitution, preferring either the chaos of the legislative branch or the confines of the executive branch. I had to admit that I was an Article II kind of guy.

The Harlow Miracle

If my first "Washington Miracle" was Malcom Moos adding me, an unemployed twenty-five-year-old, to the White House staff behind the back of Sherman Adams, the second was Bryce Harlow surprising me with an offer of a quick escape from my Senate mistake.

He must have been watching me. We did not work together at the White House, where Bryce headed up Ike's congressional relations staff. Our only conversations had been casual stuff in the White House Staff Mess. He had come to Washington from Oklahoma before World War II to work for his district's representative, served during the war on General Persons's staff at the Pentagon, then returned to Congress as the chief clerk of the House Armed Services Committee. In Eisenhower's retirement, Bryce was his most trusted political adviser. His day job was directing government relations for Procter & Gamble, but he clearly was the go-to guy for everything Republican in Washington, akin to the role Robert Strauss played for the Democrats.

Bryce was a bit over five feet tall, his voice a notch above a whisper. It was necessary to lean across the table to catch his exegeses on how government worked. His incredible skill as a negotiator related to his ability to ensure, if possible, that everyone would be able to claim some victory, plus an unassuming nature that let others claim credit. The sign in his White House office asked, "Have you come with the solution or are you part of the problem?" What made him so special to me was how he reported each side accurately to the other, made no cutting comments in drawing rooms or gossip columns, and never called into question an opponent's motives.

Bryce's job offer was simple and basic: Would I answer Eisenhower's mail? As an aside, he also asked me to be helpful to Nixon, now that the former vice president had no representation in Washington.

Laws today give former presidents such necessities as offices and staff and transportation and security. There were no such benefits in Eisenhower's era. Ike, who in retirement preferred to be called "General," simply got in his 1955 Chrysler Imperial and was driven eighty miles home to Gettysburg, Pennsylvania, escorted by a lone Secret Service vehicle, which then made a U-turn and headed back to Washington. What Bryce told me was that to keep Ike "alive" for the party's purposes, someone had to answer his mail. The Republican National Committee would pay. Would I be interested? Sure! It was better than writing in praise of California's fruits and nuts.

We had no idea how many letters there would be, so we agreed to a piecework contract. I rented office space in a Republican PR firm, hired Ann Parsons, one of Mrs. Eisenhower's secretaries, an ideal associate, and put together a large loose-leaf notebook of stock responses:

> *I regret to advise you that the General has made it a rule not to give his endorsement to candidates for school offices.*

> *General Eisenhower asked me to reply to your letter of _____ (insert date). He appreciates your thought of him. As you requested, I am glad to send you the enclosed picture that bears the General's signature.*

> *The General would have me advise you that he has in the past advocated the eighteen-year voting age on the theory that those old enough to be called into the military service of our country should have a vote.*

> *The General is glad to hear of your interest in a career in the _____ (Army/Navy/Air Force). He wishes you much success. Unfortunately, I regret that the General's heavy schedule at the present time prevents him from writing a letter of recommendation. However, I am sure that Congressman _____ (check district) will give every consideration to your application for appointment to the Academy.*

What we had not known (or imagined) was the bulk of incoming mail. There would be a deluge. The five-star general and two-term president must have been the most loved man in the world. Everyone seemed to want his autograph or a photograph or something of his for a church auction or his answer to that year's collegiate debate topic or his presence as a speaker or a letter for an aunt's eightieth birthday (she had been a great supporter in Iowa) or just to say hello. At first I thought of invent-

Mr. Stephen H. Hess
Stephen Hess Associates
Suite 700
1710 H ... N. W.
... D. C.

OFFICE OF
DWIGHT D. EISENHOWER

Gettysburg, Pennsylvania
29 June 1962

Dear Steve:

According to previous conversations, I am
forwarding to you herewith:

1. 288 facsimile autograph cards-- Dwight D. Eisenhower
2. Two binders containing names and
   numbers of correspondents in which
   the Secret Service are interested.
   These books are to be regarded as
   confidential.
3. Pictures of Mrs. Eisenhower (80)
4. In response to your query concernin...
   the person interested in donating c...
   paign buttons and the like to the N...
   suggest that J. Earl Endacott, E...
   Director, The Eisenhower Mus...
   Kansas be contacted.—

Cordially,

[signature]
ROBERT L. SCH...
Colonel, U. S. ...
Aide to General ...

Mr. Stephen Hess
1625 Eye Street, Northwest
Washington 6, D. C.

Enclosures

DDE

GETTYSBURG
PENNSYLVANIA

August 7, 1961.

Dear Steve:

Thanks again for your helpfulness. I am delighted
to have your August third fact sheet on legislation;
it has already proved most helpful to me.

With the hope that all is going well with you, and
with warm regard,

Sincerely,

D.E.

Mr. Stephen Hess,
1710 H Street, N. W.,
Washington 6, D. C.

ing a person to sign the letters so that I would not become involved in long correspondence with people who felt they had a great deal to say to Ike. But after a day, it struck me that a reporter looking for the imaginary John Doe could be a real embarrassment, and I promptly killed off my alter ego.

As we became more efficient, Ann Whitman, Eisenhower's secretary, and her staff gladly passed along more responsibility. In August 1962, I wrote to my bosses at the RNC:

1. Gettysburg now sends all mail unopened to this office (via Trailways). There is no longer any advance screening.

2. Letters are then opened and sorted, with certain categories being sent directly to the Abilene Library.

3. Letters are then screened, using Secret Service files, and certain letters are sent directly to the Secret Service.

4. All finished letters are now signed, stuffed, and ready for franking when they arrive at Gettysburg.

We started by charging $3 per letter, but eventually divided mail into three categories: $3.00 letters, $1.50 letters, and $1.00 letters, with a secretarial charge for the longer $3.00 letters. Our bill that August was for 974 letters. A shock was how many threatening letters went to the Secret Service. I had spent over two years innocently walking through the White House without ever having to show identification. This was the first time I realized the world I considered normal could be dangerous.

With so much money coming in—money that was going to redirect my life—I began providing a couple of additional services. One was to write and distribute a sort of Washington political newsletter with a circulation of two—Ike and Dick. It consisted of "brief notes" that would keep my readers connected to what was happening in Washington: "Forward momentum at Republican National Committee is grinding to a halt. Necessary decisions are being held in abeyance. The problem is the absence of Chairman Thurston Morton, whose Senate seat is up in 1962. Morton has barely and rarely been at RNC HQ of late."

The other addition was to keep track of those I knew to have connections with Eisenhower or Nixon, and to prepare brief notes they might wish to send (congratulations on being named Virginia Republican Woman of the Year, on receiving an honorary degree, on weddings and births—that sort of thing). Eisenhower was comfortable with my suggestions. (His thanks changed from "Mr. Hess" to "Steve.") He occasionally signed a note, changed his mind, crossed out his signature, and sent it back to me. (Later I asked John Eisenhower if I could give these drafts to charities; he agreed.) I was pleased when people started to tell me, "I just got the nicest note from Ike."

The Nixon part of Bryce's request was more complicated.

Working for Richard Nixon

I did not know Ike's vice president. The reason, I think, was that Eisenhower had a view of the vice presidency that is now at least a half century out of date. As Ike wrote in his memoirs, "The Vice President of the United States, with the constitutional duty of presiding over the Senate, is not legally a part of the Executive branch and is not subject to direction by the President." He even included Nixon as part of a group coming to a White House meeting as coming "from the Senate." Since Eisenhower considered the vice presidency to be in the legislative branch, everything Nixon did for him he claimed was on "a volunteer basis," including being his personal representative abroad and chairing a committee to end discrimination in government contracting.

The vice president was housed at the Capitol, as was his staff, and their paychecks came from the Senate budget. Although he was at the White House for meetings of the cabinet, National Security Council, and legislative leaders, I do not remember him as a presence in the West

Wing. He did not have a White House office as vice presidents have had since Walter Mondale served as Carter's vice president.

I first met Nixon in the spring of 1961. Visiting Washington, he borrowed a desk in the law office of Bill Rogers, his old friend who had been Eisenhower's attorney general. Nixon was now a "rainmaker" in a Los Angeles law firm. I think he liked my chatty newsletters. He missed the political gossip that had fueled his life in Washington for fourteen years. This was not the gossip of California. He later told me, "If I have to play golf one more time with Randy Scott [the cowboy movie star], I may go out of my mind." The only question I recall him asking me that day: Was I Phi Beta Kappa? I had never been asked before. (There is an unverified Nixon story that he had worried about the competition at Duke Law School after counting thirty-two PBK keys in his class. He ultimately finished third in the class.) My answer seemed important to him. He wanted my help with articles he was to write for the *Saturday Evening Post* and the Los Angeles Times Syndicate.

After we discussed the articles, he said, "Incidentally, don't send me those draft letters. I don't want to be one of those politicians who remembers people's birthdays." In any memoir some words are recalled *sort of*; these words are remembered *exactly*. Nixon had been put on the 1952 ticket because he was a politician and Eisenhower was not. Had he changed? Was there a "New Nixon"? Yet immediately after he returned to California, he wrote, "I particularly appreciate receiving the suggested drafts for letters. . . . I hope you will continue to forward such suggestions because that way I get information which is not carried in the papers here. (For example, Fritz Mueller's impending marriage.)" Are the two statements in context or in conflict? I don't know. I would have to decide whether this man was more nuanced than the Herblock cartoon I had had in my head since college.

There would be a profound difference in my writing experiences for Eisenhower and Nixon. In the White House my work was filtered through Mac Moos. The president used my words, as I have illustrated, and that was gratifying, but essentially I was a part of the process. I saw only secondhand how the president moved around our words, added and deleted, to shape the points he wished to make. Now, with Nixon, it was just the two of us. I think this was the setting in which he was most comfortable, whether it was with writers or others. I discovered how much I enjoyed this collaboration. We were not equal partners: I was there to help him, we listened to each other, he paid me. Moreover, he was excessively generous, often splitting large fees. We never negotiated. Once I told him he was paying me too much. He was embarrassed. "I'd only have to give it to the IRS," he said.

Our collegial experience was especially satisfying in 1961 when his articles were important in reintroducing him after the 1960 defeat. A magazine article (or, I assume, a law brief) was a perfect setting for his logical mind. I think he took pride in some of his *Saturday Evening Post*–length pieces, less so in what he did in a newspaper column, which I think he considered an expanded headline.

Some politicians whose positions require that they must have ghost-writers are often uncomfortable being fed words that are not their own or think they could have done better themselves if they had just had the time. It is a tale that is both funny and sad in Barton Swaim's book, *The Speechwriter*, about working for a governor of South Carolina. This was not Nixon's way. He admired writers and was a good reader. I still remember a conversation we had about *When the Cheering Stopped*, Gene Smith's account of the last years of Woodrow Wilson. Writing *Six Crises*, his episodic and compelling account of his political career from the Alger Hiss case in 1949 through losing the presidency in 1960, Nixon told me, was one of the most difficult tasks he ever attempted. Nixon's problem was that he could never have the perfect speechwriter to fit his changing moods. His attempted solution when he reached the White House was to create a troika of Ray Price (liberal), Pat Buchanan (conservative), and Bill Safire (centrist). He kept making additions, some very talented, as Robert Schlesinger points out in *White House Ghosts: Presidents and Their Speechwriters*, but ultimately he would fall back on his big three.

California, 1962

Nixon convened a small meeting at the Waldorf Towers in New York City in 1961 to hear what his key supporters from the 1960 campaign thought about whether he should run for governor of California. Perhaps a half dozen or so attended, mostly Wall Street and national politics figures. I do not know why he asked me to be there. Their analysis, in social science terms, rested on two data points: one, Nixon had carried California in 1960, surely he would win running for a lesser office in 1962; and two, public opinion polls had him comfortably ahead of the incumbent governor, Pat Brown. Otherwise the group did not seem to have more than a newspaper reader's knowledge of California politics. Their passion was playing for a presidential nomination. They wanted Nixon to be their horse—and there was already a starting gate, even if the next race was not for three years. Winning is all that matters to those who bet on politics at this level; there is no place or show. But other contenders were already lining up—Nelson Rockefeller, George Romney, perhaps William Scranton. Nixon would need the backing of those in the room. He was the only "potential president" in the Republican ranks who was not a multimillionaire. Even his modest secretaries-and-researchers operation must have outside funding. They argued that to win in 1964, he had to win in 1962. There could be no sabbatical in this contest. Nixon, however, knew there was an overriding argument against their governor-in-1962, president-in-1964 scenario, but did not wish to share it with them: namely, he would not be able to defeat John Kennedy. Incumbent presidents rarely lose. Some Republican was going to have to be the sacrificial lamb, and Nixon was going to make sure he was not it. If he had been unable to beat Senator Kennedy in 1960, when holding the more advantageous position, he was not going to beat President Kennedy in 1964.

On September 27, 1961, Nixon held a press conference in Los Angeles to announce that he would be a candidate for governor of California in 1962 and would *not* be a candidate for president of the United States in 1964. It was easy to divine Nixon's thinking. By committing himself to serving the people of California for four years, in 1964 he would be able to appreciate the exhortations from national Republican leaders who would urge him to come to the aid of the party yet still reject them because he was honor-bound to fulfill his promise to California voters. Nixon's strategy is, importantly, about sidestepping the Kennedys. The Twenty-second Amendment would prohibit President Kennedy from running for a third term—and in 1968, Richard Nixon would be available and only fifty-five years old.

During the 1962 campaign, Governor Brown's ads proclaimed that Nixon wanted to "double-park in Sacramento" on his way back to Washington. The slogan had a nice ring to it, and it polled well—even though it fundamentally mischaracterized what Nixon was doing. Poor Richard Nixon was looking for a place to hide, not park, and no one believed him.

I moved to Los Angeles in April to work through the June primary. I returned once during the summer for the state convention, and then stayed in California from Labor Day through Election Day. Nixon's prospects looked different when viewed up close. California Republican politics, I discovered, was more brutal than I had imagined. As I wrote later with David Broder in *The Republican Establishment*:

> When Big Bill Knowland came charging home from Washington in 1958, intent on wresting the governorship from [Goodwin] Knight as a launching pad for his presidential ambitions, he triggered a chain reaction of seriocomic catastrophes: Knowland bumped Knight into the Senate primary, where Knight bumped San Francisco Mayor George Christopher. Both Knowland and Knight then were mauled in the general election, and Pat Brown, the inoffensive son of a poker-parlor operator, became Governor by a million votes. The Democrats gained control of the legislature for the first time since 1888. . . . Defeat opened the ideological floodgates. So long as they were the party of government, the Republicans had remained in touch with reality. . . . [Now] the G.O.P. entered a whirlpool of extremism.

Nixon's opponent in the gubernatorial primary was Joseph Shell—a former USC football star, oil millionaire, and now the conservative minority leader in the California State Assembly. He had no chance of winning, but the third of the vote he would receive was a serious warning to someone of Nixon's stature. The leading issue was Shell's support by the ideologically extreme John Birch Society, whose founder, Robert Welch, had accused Eisenhower of being a "conscious agent of the Communist conspiracy." Nixon repudiated Welch and the John Birch Society, as expected—but he also repudiated all candidates who would not repudiate the society, including two friends in Congress, John Rousselot and Edgar Hiestand, who represented heavily Republican districts—a move that further cut into his vote. (In his race for governor in 1966, Ronald Reagan would also oppose the John Birch Society, but—with more skill—he would tell other candidates they were on their own.) On one occasion Nixon was shaving just before we went out to dinner. He was in his office's private bathroom, talking to me through the open door. "I could not look myself in the mirror if I support them," he told me. I could see his image through the mirror and wondered for a moment if this was a set piece. No, he had no need to impress me. Nixon was reassuring Nixon. Even now I think it was the attack on Eisenhower that so bothered Nixon, though other politicians took it less seriously.

Running for governor of California was not like running for president writ small. Rather, it was more like being moved from first class to the back of coach flying from Washington to Los Angeles. Where are the complimentary beverages before takeoff? The attendant offering to hang up your coat? Or the roomier seats and hot towels? Nixon probably did not notice. But traveling with him now meant there were fewer of us— usually the always present Rose Mary Woods, a press aide (either Sandy Quinn or Ron Ziegler), an all-purpose advance man, and me—doing more things that were not in our job descriptions. For example, one time Rose got my attention: Steve, there is a man in the lobby who insists Nixon must deal with the great injustice that has befallen him. Could you talk to him? The great injustice, it turned out, was that he had been convicted of embezzling from his daughter, a well-known movie actress.

Nor was this a one-stop-a-day campaign, more like breakfast meeting in Los Angeles, luncheon speech in San Francisco, evening rally in San Diego, back to bed where you started in Los Angeles. We entrusted driving to local volunteers, one of whom went the wrong way on a freeway as oncoming cars sought paths to avoid a high-speed collision. Nixon and speechwriter survive for another rally! My daily exercise was a thirty-minute walk in the morning from my motel on Olympic Boulevard to Nixon's downtown office, shedding tears along the way (due less to the stress of the campaign than to LA's poisonous smog).

California is a massive state then on the brink of becoming the most populous in the nation, and, Nixon being Nixon, he traveled it all, shaking lines of hands, 500 in Chico, each handshake coming with a few upbeat words, perhaps sounding as if he were greeting a lifelong friend. (At one stop I remember standing behind him thinking, "Is this the introvert I used to know?") We soldiered on. It was the only time in my life I recognized a condition called bone-weary. A photograph I cherish shows me sound asleep, Nixon coming down the plane's aisle with a look suggesting that I was about to get another assignment.

Nixon was buoyed by the crowds. It was an unrealistic gauge. The crowds were there to see half of the "Kennedy/Nixon" team. They wanted to meet a celebrity, not a California politician. Still, it would be wrong, as Nixon might have said, to consider the campaign a joyless experience for the campaigners. I know I loved being tested. Moreover, there were two parts of the campaign that were genuinely meant to be fun—the whistle-stop tour and the telethon.

The Whistle-Stop Tour

On October 18, less than three weeks before the election, Dick and Pat Nixon boarded an eight-car train for a three-day trip down the California coast. Nixon was not exactly making political history with this whistle-stop tour—it had nothing on Harry Truman's historic 31,000-mile, 352-speech trip to a surprise victory in 1948—but it was the best I would ever experience firsthand. Car 8 was a Pullman coach for the press. Working forward from there was a chair car for general use; a tavern and lounge car for the reporters, many of whom had flown in from Washington; a reception lounge for local officials; a Pullman coach for staff; and the open-end observation car called an "Airslie," from which the Nixons emerged so the candidate could address the gatherers. The local politicians boarded one stop before their town to chat with Nixon. The Fullerton people got on at Pico Rivera and traveled eleven miles to Fullerton, where they were replaced on board by the Anaheim people. The steady pace added drama: rallies on the first day in Santa Cruz at 8:30 a.m., Watsonville at 9:55, Salinas at 10:45, King City at 11:55, Paso Robles at a quarter past one in the afternoon, San Luis Obispo at 2:45. Then, after switching tracks, it was on to Santa Maria at 4:40, an off-train rally in Santa Barbara at 7:50, then a departure for Los Angeles at 9:30 p.m. On October 19, at 6:30 a.m., breakfast service began. Each stop wanted to be special: a cowboy band in Salinas, a Dixieland jazz band in Fullerton, a gift to the Nixons of a box of something—apples, tomatoes, almonds, strawberries, greens. The most famous legend of the trip is that the Democratic prankster Dick Tuck, wearing a conductor's hat, waved the train forward as Nixon was speaking. Good story, but it never happened.

The Telethon

The telethon was supposed to offer an evening's home entertainment as the candidate took on all challengers. In 1960, on the eve of the November 8 election, Nixon managed to squeeze in a four-hour national telethon broadcast on ABC after flying overnight from Alaska on his way to Chicago. Now, in California, he was going to use the telethon technique in an even bigger way. There were to be seven of them, held during prime time over the last several weeks of the campaign. The final two were scheduled for San Francisco, on October 22, and Los Angeles, on November 3, with earlier multiple-community saturations in Salinas-Monterey-San Luis Obispo, on September 28, and Sacramento-Chico-Eureka, on October 16. The format called for questions to be phoned in from local audiences and read to the candidate on camera by celebrities. In fact, the questions were first detoured to me. My job was to turn "Mr.

Nixon, what is your view on communism?" into "Mr. Nixon, why do the Communists hate you so much?" The celebrity would then say, "Here's a real tough one, Dick." A problem, however, was that Nixon's celebrities were long in the tooth—Cesar Romero, Constance Moore, Dennis Morgan, Rhonda Fleming, Victor Jory, Jeannette MacDonald, Lloyd Nolan, and John Payne, five of whom were born before 1910. Strangely, we only needed a hook for three of our younger stars: Gale Storm (*My Little Margie*), too flirtatious for Nixon; Johnny Mathis, too gay for Nixon; and Chuck Connors (*The Rifleman*), who left Nixon grasping for a response to "Me and the boys were talking about Jeffersonian democracy on the set today."

Numerous articles tell how a twenty-eight-year-old Roger Ailes gained fame as Nixon's television producer in 1968. It is less well known that six years earlier another television notable, Paul Keyes, had provided Nixon with page after page of next-day reflections on the telethons, even including how the announcer should introduce the candidate: "Once in the lifetime of every state a leader is born destined to lead his state to greatness—Ladies and gentleman, I give you the next Governor of California!"

The Paul Keyes Touch

Nixon met Paul Keyes when he appeared on the *Tonight* show with Jack Paar. Paul was a professional gag writer who would go on to write for *Rowan & Martin's Laugh-In*, a massively successful ode to silliness and one of the biggest hit TV shows of the late 1960s. The friendship of Nixon and Keyes was instant. This was not Nixon's habit—his inner circle was small and long-tested. It might be poetic to think of Paul playing Shakespeare's clown for Nixon. But this was not Paul's style, even though he did funny very well. His nearness was very good for Nixon. Good for me too, I should add, as Paul's approach to humor would come in handy when a speech called for something that was supposed to get a laugh. Paul told me about writing his first joke: it was for Rudy Vallée, the famous megaphone crooner of the 1930s, who said he needed a joke for a Madison Square Garden benefit. What kind of joke? An animal joke. On a sheet of paper, Paul made a list of all the animals that came to mind, and then, in an adjacent column, a list of each animal's most notable characteristic—stripes for tigers, humps for camels, elephants' tusks. This was the joke: A mother kangaroo said to another, "Don't you hate these rainy days when the kids can't go out and play?"

I never wrote any jokes for Nixon, whose humor at that time was mostly about "going to the Electoral College and having flunked debating." Still, Paul's lessons later came in handy when, in January 1965, Gerald Ford became the new Republican leader in Congress and Bryce Harlow (of course!) asked me to write an introductory speech Ford was to deliver at the National Press Club in Washington. The substance of the speech was okay; the problem was that I did not *know* Ford. So I wrote down all the characteristics I could think of, such as his being a football star at the University of Michigan. My solution for Ford's opener was this: "I wonder where I would be today if I had accepted Curly Lambeau's offer to play for the Green Bay Packers." Then, after a long pause: "Perhaps on the Supreme Court!" Since President Kennedy had just nominated Byron "Whizzer" White—a former All-American halfback at the University of Colorado—to the Supreme Court, the Press Club's insiders were primed to laugh. One more attempt at a joke for Ford came when he was invited to speak at an Israel bond rally in Chicago. Here I tried to tease a string of Israeli-Republican similarities, ending with Senator Everett McKinley Dirksen of Illinois and Prime Minister David Ben-Gurion of Israel using the same hair stylist. I heard that Ford liked my jokes more than my substance; otherwise he was a very nice man—and nice to me.

Paul Keyes, by my calculation, deserves to be among a small group that can take credit for Nixon's 1968 presidential victory. The catchphrase of *Laugh-In*, Paul's program, was "sock it to me," a line that took a second to say and was then repeated by millions of viewers each week. On September 16, 1968, less than two months before the presidential election, Paul Keyes convinced Nixon to do the bit. Nixon turned the phrase into an incredulous question—"Sock it to meeee?" Of all the manufactured efforts to create the New Nixon that Joe McGinniss documented in *The Selling of the President,* none created a more likable image of the Republican candidate than "Sock it to meeee?"

The last time I recall seeing Paul was at a Gridiron Dinner in Washington. The shows are put on by a club of veteran journalists wearing outrageous costumes and singing their own lyrics to popular songs. Between the reporters' skits were various meant-to-be funny speeches, one by the president or his representative. In 1969 the speaker was Vice President Spiro Agnew, whose limitations in the humor department were well known. Yet his speech was hilarious. I particularly liked Agnew explaining how well the president was treating him. "He even gives me my own plane," he chimed. "Air Force 13. . . . It's a glider."

Who wrote it, I wondered? Then I saw Paul Keyes in the audience.

"Paul," I said, "you wrote a terrific speech!"

"I didn't write it," he said. This was what speechwriters are supposed to say.

"The only trouble, Paul, was that it was a little long."

"You should have seen the first draft."

Paul Keyes died on January 2, 2004. He was seventy-nine years old.

Governor Brown's Speech

Nixon once attributed his loss in the 1962 California gubernatorial race to the Cuban missile crisis, but there were more immediate reasons why voters rejected the former vice president. Californians had concluded that Pat Brown was a good governor, though he did not necessarily look like one, or sometimes even sound like one. But he had a worthy record—and I should know, since I wrote it for him! Nixon and Brown were to have only one debate, sponsored by UPI, on October 1 in San Francisco. Each candidate was to get a seven-minute opening statement. On September 29, Nixon sent me ahead to San Francisco with instructions to write what I thought his opponent would say. He did not wish to be surprised. I called Agnes Waldron, Nixon's chief researcher in Los Angeles, and requested copies of all of Governor Brown's speeches. My hunch was that rather than write a new speech, Brown would deliver the "Best of Brown" (which is what I would have done for Nixon), and so

I would put together the governor's remarks with tape and scissors. My version of Governor Brown's opening remarks told of "three new university campuses, six new state college campuses and a medical school, . . . a water program which will control floods in the north and carry surplus water to the Central Valley and the south, . . . the first Office of Consumer Counsel to protect our families from fraud in the marketplace," and so on. I did not tell Nixon that I had borrowed Brown's speech from Brown. All he knew was that the Brown speech I gave him that night, almost word for word, was what Brown would say tomorrow. Nixon's opinion of Hess gained great altitude that day.

There is yet another "event" that helps explain how we underestimated our opponent.

The Nixons had moved into the Trousdale Estates section of Beverly Hills. The house was not a mansion, but it must have been expensive, given their movie star neighbors. To me as an Easterner, it was reminiscent of upper-middle-class Scarsdale. Nixon loved it. For him it was an affirmation of having made it—of having pulled himself up (as was his Oldsmobile convertible). On my first two visits, I got a tour of the place, during which Nixon said, "On a clear day you can see Catalina." (It was apparently never clear enough when I was there.) My third visit was with Paul Keyes, who made a joke of the Catalina line, and we never heard of Catalina again. On that Sunday I gathered with Nixon's veterans—Bob Haldeman, Bob Finch, Herb Klein—to hear Governor Brown on a "meet the press"–type program. Nixon himself did not watch, only coming into the den for our judgments. We were united and harsh—on the governor's mumbling, of missing this point, of getting that fact wrong. Then my favorite Nixon, fourteen-year-old Julie, burst into the room to tell us we were all wrong—Pat Brown was "terrific," she said. She was right, of course.

Nevertheless, Nixon might have won had he been able to convince Californians he wanted to be their governor, and why. Instead, Nixon wrote in his memoir, "I was really not all that eager to be governor of California." California's concerns—schools and taxes and highways and water and recreation—were not particularly Nixon's, as would be evident from the issues he chose and did not choose to emphasize. Eisenhower had urged him to run, but to Nixon, Sacramento was "so far away from the centers of national and international news media that I simply do not believe it would be possible for me . . . to speak at all constructively." He added, "My entire experience in government has been in national and international affairs. I think the problems which governors have to handle are immensely important but my interests simply are in other fields." This was true. Even in the middle of the governor's race he found ways to reference world events. Perhaps he thought it was good politics to remind voters of his breadth. But I think not. It was just where his mind was. As I had Pat Brown say in my UPI debate draft, "Mr. Nixon will find that the people want a governor who is more interested in Agriculture than in Afghanistan." Nixon's favorite "local issue" was communists teaching in California schools.

Cuban Missiles

On October 22, President Kennedy addressed the nation from the Oval Office: "This government, as promised, has maintained the closest surveillance of the Soviet military buildup on the island of Cuba."

Three of us were listening from a hotel room in Oakland—me, Rose Mary Woods, and Richard Nixon:

> Within the past week, unmistakable evidence has established the fact that a series of offensive missile sites is now in preparation on that imprisoned island. The purpose of these bases can be none other than to provide a nuclear strike capability against the Western Hemisphere. . . . It shall be the policy of this nation to regard any nuclear missile launched from Cuba against any nation in the Western Hemisphere as an attack by the Soviet Union on the United States, requiring a full retaliatory response to the Soviet Union.

Nixon turned to me and said, "I just lost the election."

His reaction was instantaneous, reflexive. Later, there would be a release of emotion. But at that exact moment, his comment was without affect—simply a matter-of-fact statement of fact.

I was confused. "What's this got to do with you?" I asked.

Nixon explained, "There's no way that anyone is going to pay any attention to a California governor's race now."

This future was not shared with the staff. Instead, we continued on to San Diego. The campaign bought statewide TV time for the following night. Nixon gave an address in support of the president's action. The world waited nervously for Soviet leader Nikita Khrushchev's response to President Kennedy's challenge. There was really nothing else to say.

Fifty-five years later, I remember I was there in a still Oakland hotel room as Richard Nixon, two years removed from being defeated for president of the United States, watched John Kennedy, the man who defeated him, speaking the most important words of his presidency.

"My Last Press Conference"

On the morning of November 7, the day after Richard Nixon lost to Pat Brown by 297,000 votes, the defeated candidate met with reporters:

> Now that all the members of the press are so delighted that I lost, I would just like to make a statement of my own. . . . For sixteen years, ever since the Hiss case, you've had a lot of fun—a lot of fun—that you've had an opportunity to attack me, and I think I've given as good as I've taken. . . . I leave you gentlemen now, and you will now write it. You will interpret it. That's your right. But as I leave you I want you to know—just think how much you're going to be missing me. . . . You won't have Nixon to kick around anymore, because, gentlemen, this is my last press conference.

I was not in the room. I heard these bitter, angry words as I was waking up in the motel on Olympic Boulevard. I went home that day, back to Washington, and never mentioned the "last press conference" to Nixon.

I was surprised, but not shocked. It was hardly news that Nixon hated the press. But more than many politicians of that time—only a third of U.S. senators even had a press secretary—Nixon had a firm sense of how news is produced, from deadlines to pecking orders, and could sometimes use this to advantage. From the Alger Hiss days, he had always played a few favorites. The California reporters covering him in 1962 were well within the circle of competence that was his experience. Herb Klein, Sandy Quinn, and young Ron Ziegler worked hard to keep them as informed as they had a right to be.

Nixon's problem in press relations was Nixon himself, not the reporters. At the beginning of the campaign we had convinced Nixon to throw a party for the reporters. A ballroom, plenty of good food and drink. The reporters gathered round, and Nixon began telling a story. "If you want a fresh salad in a restaurant, ask the waiter to slice the tomato against the grain." That's Nixon's story. His awkward attempt at small talk left the reporters stunned. (Explanation: As a kid Nixon worked in a restaurant's kitchen where salads were prepared, with tomatoes sliced with the grain, three hours before the guests arrived.)

Nixon called me on Election Day morning, November 6, to say good-bye and to thank me for my help. We were not planning to meet that day. I asked him if he still thought he was going to lose. "Yes," he answered, "but at least I am never going to have to talk about crap like dope addiction anymore." I wrote a short concession statement in case he might want something to say and dropped it off at headquarters. What would be the next life for this man who had been so close to being the President of the United States? On November 15, back in Washington, I wrote Nixon:

Dear Dick:

I've been trying to unwind by reading some history. I'm struck by the career of William Seward, who, as you will recall, deserved to be the first Republican President. Of course he was thwarted by Lincoln, but went on to become a great Secretary of State. At any rate, there are many productive years ahead and my hope is that you will concentrate them on international affairs. Perhaps in six or eight months you might consider a world trip which would produce a series of articles and a book. My feeling is that your future should be as nonpolitical as possible.

Clearly, I had concluded that the double defeat, 1960 and 1962, with the latter more devastating than the former, had ended Nixon's career in elective politics, moreover even without yet knowing that he was going to move to New York, Nelson Rockefeller's territory. How little I understood him! The goal of being president of the United States, no matter how unrealistic, was bedrock Nixon, as I would learn before too long.

November 22, 1963

It was Friday. I was in New York City to meet with Richard Nixon in mid-afternoon when he returned from Dallas, where he had attended a board meeting of Pepsi-Cola, one of his law firm's clients.

Nixon had asked if I would help him write a book. It was Paul Keyes's idea. Nixon, the insider's insider, would challenge Theodore White by telling the story of the 1964 presidential election. White's *The Making of the President, 1960* was the greatest political book I had ever read, taking readers backstage where they had never been before. Among those of us who wrote about politics, it was revolutionary. I loved the possibilities of Nixon versus White. White's book had been at the top of the best-seller list for all of 1961; the only other book so rewarded was the New English Bible. Ken McCormick, editor in chief of Doubleday, had told us he was very enthusiastic and would make a firm offer the following Monday.

In the middle of a leisurely lunch at Monsignor's with Ellin Roberts, my editor at Doubleday, our waiter, who spoke English with a heavy Italian accent, came over to the table and said, "Kennedy dead." Was this a joke? Ellin and I took off down Fifth Avenue to seek confirmation, which we got in a Magnavox showroom. John F. Kennedy, thirty-fifth president of the United States, had been assassinated while riding in a motorcade in Dallas, Texas.

I called Nixon's Wall Street law office. It was now about a quarter past two. Nixon had just returned. He had heard the news when his cab from the airport stopped at a red light in Queens. I was to go directly to his home on Fifth Avenue at 62nd Street.

Nixon greeted me at the front door of his apartment. His jacket was off, but he was still wearing a tie. He appeared shaken. His daughters were home, glued to the television. He told them it could have been him (even though in his memoirs he will write that he "never felt the 'there but for the grace of God go I' reaction").

He showed me his interview in the previous day's *Dallas Morning News*. We were still standing in the front hall. He had urged the city to give Kennedy "a courteous reception"—the reference was to a recent incident in Dallas when Adlai Stevenson was heckled and spat upon. This was not the way people should disagree in a democracy, Nixon said; we must show respect for political adversaries. Why does he quote from this article now, I wondered? Perhaps it was an unspoken "See, I didn't encourage this terrible act!"

We moved into the den, where he called J. Edgar Hoover to ask if the killer was a right-winger. That was an important point to him. No, said the director of the FBI, he was a communist with a connection to Castro. (How quickly they know!) This was a relief. Nixon then called Eisenhower at the Waldorf, where the former president was taking a nap, and was told that Eisenhower would return the call later.

We were joined by Paul Keyes and Rose Mary Woods. A short statement had to be made for the media. TV cameras were already in front of the building. Nixon would tell of his friendship with Kennedy when they were both freshman members of the House of Representatives. Rose had to clear his schedule to go to the funeral. He was to have played golf the following day with Roger Blough, president of U.S. Steel, then take in a white-tie evening at the opera with Tom Dewey. All speeches were canceled for a month.

The conversation moved to political consequences. Nixon said he thought there would be a bloodletting between Lyndon Johnson and

Bobby Kennedy for the Democratic nomination. Maybe Adlai Stevenson would emerge as a compromise. I stayed at the apartment until about half past six.

The next day, Saturday, the politicos were already at the Nixon apartment paying respect to the man who three years ago had almost defeated Jack Kennedy. Former National Republican Committee chairman Len Hall was there; Cliff Folger, the 1960 finance chairman, was on the phone. Nixon said that, after thinking about it, he now felt that the Democrats would unite behind Johnson. They agreed that the assassination greatly weakened Goldwater. Nixon was convinced he would probably be back in the race for the presidency.

His book about the 1964 presidential election would never be written. I headed back home to Washington, a city now in mourning.

A Bookmaker

With my wealth from answering Eisenhower's letters, and the generosity of Nixon for assisting with his articles, I was able to return to Washington and turn to the writing I really wanted to do. I had enough money not to have to make money for almost three years. I set up an office in the attic of our Cleveland Park house, removed from the rest of the family. I had two IBM Selectric typewriters, bought for $50 each at the going-out-of-business sale of the Nixon-Lodge 1960 presidential campaign. I bought a recently invented portable copying machine (portable if you had the strength to carry around fifteen pounds). The copying machine shone light through the document onto a sheet of chemically coated paper, which then tended to curl and slowly fade. Within a few years all of this would be replaced by xerography.

Our house shared a double driveway. When a Swiss family moved in next door, on a pleasant spring day in 1966, I overheard this bit of conversation through my open third-floor window:

Swiss boy: My daddy is a diplomat.

Charlie Hess, age five: My daddy is a bookmaker.

Bookmaker, a maker of books. The plural, in fact, was fitting. I was in the process of writing three books, and soon there would be a fourth.

I had already published *Hats in the Ring: The Making of Presidential Candidates* in 1960, a collaboration with Malcolm Moos that had started as a public television series when he was a professor and I was a student. When we became White House speechwriters, publishers became interested, as did White House reporters, whose reviews found value I had not imagined.

The second book was my overriding ambition. *America's Political Dynasties: From Adams to Kennedy* grew out of the genealogical notes I had brought back from my military nights in the United States Information Service library in Frankfurt, Germany.

The third book was a stepchild of the first. The problem with *Hats in the Ring* was that the manuscript was truly thin, at least in terms of length. So I set off to the Library of Congress to add bulk with appropriate cartoons from its collection, where I was befriended by Milton Kaplan, curator of historical prints, who convinced me that the world did not have but badly needed a history of American political cartoons. This need we—Milton and I—ultimately filled with *The Ungentlemanly Art: A History of American Political Cartoons,* published by Macmillan in 1968. One of the joys of writing this book was putting cartoons in the footnotes to illustrate the purpose of the footnote. "Most enjoyable footnotes I've ever seen," wrote the reviewer in *Journalism Quarterly.*

My fourth book grew out of my concerns about the Republican Party after the Goldwater disaster of 1964. The candidate's swift move to the right produced one of the most lopsided defeats in the history of the republic. No editor at Random House, the publisher to which I contractually owed a book, had any interest in editing a book about Republicans, but an editor at Random House knew an editor at Harper & Row. (I was starting to learn things about this industry.) When I realized that my ambition for this project exceeded the time I was given and the scope I desired, I sought out my friend Dave Broder of the *Washington Post*, who also wanted to be a bookmaker. Thus we collaborated on *The Republican Establishment: The Present and Future of the G.O.P.*, which Harper & Row published in 1967. This was my perfect collaboration: I could hardly tell which words were mine and which were Dave's. When he died at the age of eighty-one in 2011, he had long been recognized as the nation's leading political reporter. In a column titled "Why We Loved David Broder," E. J. Dionne wrote, "To the extent that David had an ideology, it was a bias toward nonpartisan problem-solving. It was why, I think, he was so interested in moderate Republicans in the 1960s."

My fifth book was *Nixon: A Political Portrait*, published by Harper & Row in 1968. This book resulted from an agreement with a friend, Earl Mazo, who had written a very good Nixon biography in 1959 and was not in position to revise it. The 1968 *Nixon* was half new (Hess) and half from the original (Mazo). The authors later learned that the 1968 campaign scrapped thousands of copies of the book because Rose Mary Woods and Bob Haldeman felt the sketch of Nixon on the cover looked too severe.

This unexpected publishing history, four books released by major publishers in three years—one in 1966, one in 1967, and two in 1968— was going to change my life in a way that producing one or even two books over the same time probably would not have. The bookmaker lives in a hard-to-be-noticed world, and I had inadvertently been dealt a four-book monte of being more visible, more often.

Go back to the beginning: getting off the troop ship at twenty-five, with only a bachelor's degree from Johns Hopkins, and then being thrust into a career of high-altitude political associations, making friends, doing favors, being helpful, not getting into trouble. The expected trajectory of success is more success. Yet what if you want to change direction? It was not as though there was anything wrong with the direction I was going in. Rather, there were other places I would rather be. What, then, were the odds of changing a reputation in midcourse?

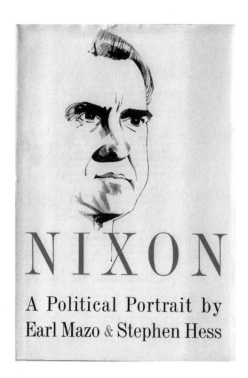

Reviewers had to like my books, of course, but they also had to serve a reputational need: Where would the literary establishment place me on their scale?

America's Political Dynasties, the first of the books in this artificial series, received a full-page review in the *New York Times Book Review* on September 4, 1966, the place to be seen. The reviewer, Henry F. Graff, a professor of history at Columbia University, had kind words for the book: "prodigious thoroughness," "masterly fashion." He also informed his readers that the book was written by "Stephen Hess, a free-lancer who served briefly as a staff assistant at the White House during the Eisenhower Administration." Is there room for a "free-lancer" in the academy? The professor's words of praise seemed to vanish with that single pinprick.

The rapid publication of the books that followed was going to influence how reviewers identified me. I had not acquired advanced degrees or other marks of academic achievement, yet over three years I had been elevated to "political scientist" by the *New Yorker* and the *New York Times* and to "political historian" by the *Boston Globe* and *Choice*. In one review I was even "a brilliant pedagogue." My most satisfying review identified me as "Mr. Hess." This is classy. Margaret L. Coit, a historian I deeply admired, wrote a lavish two-page review in the *Saturday Review*, calling attention to "the remarkable women members of the ruling class," a special theme of the *Dynasty* book that was rarely noted at that time.

During this period I organized a small group of moderate Republican congressmen for once-a-month conversations on subjects such as the negative income tax. It was paid for by a small grant I received from the Institute for Policy Studies, a new left-wing think tank that liked the idea that it could also support Republicans. There were eight of us (although usually only five were there at any one session). I provided reading material and sometimes a speaker. Alphonzo Bell of California, developer of the Bel Air neighborhood in Los Ángeles, provided the refreshment and we met late afternoons in his office. I once said to Bill Steiger of Wisconsin, my favorite in the group, that academics thought of me as a politician. He smiled. "Politicians think of you as an academic," he replied. Can life be comfortably spent between these poles? Does such a place have a name? I must think about it.

Could I position myself to become a senior fellow at the Brookings Institution? Not likely. Senior fellows are Ph.D.s. This was out of my league. *America's Political Dynasties* was never meant to be my personal doctoral dissertation. Yet I must admit there was evidence that I possessed dogged dedication to a subject: as a popular history for trade publication (as advertised), the book should have covered twelve families; I did sixteen. There was no great demand for the Tuckers of Virginia or the Stocktons of New Jersey, for instance. Fifty pages of endnotes would have been acceptable to Doubleday, yet I did ninety-two, plus appendix A ("Public Offices Held by Political Dynasties"), twenty pages long; appendix B ("Other Families in Which Three or More Members Have

Served in Congress"), forty-six pages; a bibliography, twenty-nine pages; and an index, thirty pages. Total: 736 pages.

One weekday morning during my book tour, on the kitchen-like set of *Good Morning, Chicago*, Vivian della Chiesa, the hostess, tried to pick up the book. "This is a pretty weighty tome, Mr. Hess," she quipped. "Any good sex in it?" A book about families has to have sex. I held forth until the producer had had enough. That was the day *America's Political Dynasties* sold out in Chicago.

Lincoln Week, 1966

The unwinding of politics from bookmaking reached an unexpected flash point during Lincoln Week in 1966. Every year around Lincoln's birthday Republican leaders spread out around the country to deliver inspiration at local party fundraisers. In 1966, when Nixon went forth on this annual trek, Lockheed offered to fly him on the JetStar, the same plane piloted by Pussy Galore in the James Bond picture *Goldfinger*. I asked if I could bum a ride. The trip, I thought, might produce something of interest for the book on the Republican establishment I was writing with Dave Broder. Also on the trip was John Whitaker, a geologist, who had made a hobby of being useful to Nixon. When we stopped for refueling on the way back, as Nixon and I were walking along the tarmac, Nixon asked me to move to New York to work for him. I was startled. There had been no hints. Nixon had no other political aides at that time. As flattering as the offer was, I told him that I had saved enough money to devote myself to writing books. *America's Political Dynasties* was just about finished, and I was under contract for two more books.

Returning to the plane, I mentioned our conversation to John: Nixon offered, I declined.

"This is going to change your relationship with him," John said.

"What do you mean?" I said. Nixon and I had worked together closely and, I thought, skillfully since 1961.

"You said no to him."

John understood Nixon better than I. At that moment on the tarmac, I dropped out of Nixon's inner circle.

It would take time for me to absorb not being close to Richard Nixon. It was fun having a celebrity friend. I would miss little things like eyes turning to our table in a restaurant, trying not to stare, wondering who was that man with Nixon; the chef sending over favorite dishes not on the menu—the Lanny Budd moments to savor. There was still friendship, but it would never be the same after he reached out to me and I said no.

I had seen young enthusiasts like me stay too long and turn into courtiers. In the Washington of my generation, I most associated this with the Kennedy entourage. We had been young at the same time, thrilled with the game of politics, traveling in the same circles, convinced of how smart we were. But there were differences. The Kennedy staffers put an unusual mark on the importance of whom they worked for; we merely felt we had good jobs in the right arena. They liked to be intense. We liked to be cool. One Kennedy aide went into a deep depression when he mistranslated a line of Latin for Jack. An overworked aide to Bobby fell asleep at the dinner table where I was also a guest. (We left him sleeping.) A third tracked me down at a party in desperate need of a joke for Teddy. I thought they gave up a lot.

My decision on the tarmac had consequences for Pat Buchanan. At that time, Buchanan was an editorial page writer for the St. Louis *Globe Democrat,* bombarding Nixon with clippings and entreaties on why he should become his assistant. Buchanan flew to New York for an interview and was hired. He did not know—probably still does not know—that the job was available because I had turned it down.

There were consequences for Nixon, as well: Buchanan wrote a book about Nixon's nomination and election in 1968, and how he connected Nixon to the conservative movement. The book might be over the top in self-praise, but his point was valid: his right-wing credentials were useful to Nixon. Hess would not have tried to move Nixon in that direction.

Harvard, 1967–68

Some book reviewers added to my résumé that I was a Harvard man. They were slightly right. But being a fellow at the Institute of Politics at Harvard's John F. Kennedy School of Government for the academic year 1967–68 was not like having a teaching position. Rather, I spent much of my time finishing all those books for which I had contracts. The Institute of Politics is Harvard's tribute to Kennedy the politician. I was at Harvard as a politician. I felt honored to be a Kennedy Fellow; I was delighted to be able to say that I had slept in Jack Kennedy's senior year dorm room—Suite F-14, Winthrop House; I was charmed to have tea with his widow, as beautiful in person as seen on the evening news. (I might even report that she had a run in her stockings.)

One of my new colleagues as a Kennedy Fellow was Hale Champion, who had been the state finance director under Governor Brown in California. We immediately went out for lunch to compare our 1962 campaign experiences. When the check came, he pushed it over to me. "Here, you always said I was fiscally irresponsible."

Looking back on my year at Harvard, my happiest times were spent with Professor Daniel Patrick Moynihan and his wife, Liz. I had known Pat slightly from when he had been in Washington as an assistant to Secretary of Labor Arthur Goldberg, a family friend. Goldberg, as was his way, commanded that Pat and I were to be close friends. Now, in Cambridge, we actually had the time to get to know each other, to form a bond that would last a lifetime.

Being in Cambridge as a "Nixon man" raised me to a certain notoriety, as became apparent when a famous Harvard Law School professor invited me to his elegant home for a large seated dinner. I did not know my host or the other guests except by reputation. I thought this a quite nice gesture to a newcomer. Cocktail in hand, a woman asked me a question, then cut herself off: "I'm sorry, you will probably be talking about this in your speech tonight." "My speech!" "Oh, you didn't know? Louis is so forgetful." Fortunately, at the dinner table the women seated on either side of me engaged in a nonstop conversation on Japanese culture, giving me time to prepare my remarks. *The Republican Establishment* had just been published and would be my framework for assessing party prospects in the race for president. With Harvard disdain for Lyndon Johnson and opposition to the war in Vietnam, it seemed appropriate.

The year 1968, directly or indirectly, was going to revolve around the coming presidential election.

The World Affairs Council asked me to represent Nixon in a debate before Boston high school students. Henry Kissinger spoke for Nelson Rockefeller. I limited my remarks to the one thing Nixon stood for that would appeal to this audience, his proposal to substitute an all-volunteer army for the draft. I cannot remember what Henry said but I was surprised that he was nervous; possibly he had not spent much time talking to sixteen-year-olds. I would not see him again until the Republican convention in Miami Beach in August, when, as our escalators crossed, Henry whispered the real skinny: "Rockefeller on the third ballot." Another year later, when we both had offices in President Nixon's White House, and shared adjacent urinals in the basement men's room, he leaned over to complete our Boston debate: "Steve, you were right. This is the right man for this moment in history." (The line is funnier if spoken with a German accent.)

In late February there was an unexpected call from my agent in New York: "The *Ladies' Home Journal* wants you to write an article on the courtship of Julie Nixon and David Eisenhower."

"Elizabeth, how can you ask?" I said. "I am a serious writer."

"They will pay $5,000." That was the equivalent of more than $36,000 in today's dollars—a lot of money.

Julie was a student at Smith College in Northampton, Massachusetts. "I will be on the next Peter Pan bus to Northampton," I said.

The magazine's editor gave me a list of questions that I tried to answer in the article:

—What is your earliest recollection of David?
"I remember David [in 1957] because his grandmother scolded him. He decided to take us all outside so we could play on the

[White House] grounds, and all of a sudden his grandmother came out of a door and she said, 'What are you doing out there without a coat on?'"

—First date:
David took Julie to a freshman party at Amherst. . . . "Julie and David were so engrossed in conversation that they didn't dance. . . . That night was also the first time Julie had ever hitchhiked." (This was the standard way carless Amherst boys transported Smith dates.)

—Can famous names be a nuisance?
"Once David ordered flowers by phone and had to spend 15 minutes trying to convince the florist that an *Eisenhower* really wanted the red roses to go to a *Nixon*."

—How did he propose?
"The way he proposed was so personal I just want it to be between David and me."

—Did you accept on the spot?
"Yes, I mean, I was really sure."

—On telling your father.
"I didn't tell my father until the day before Thanksgiving. I felt very shy about it, and hoped he'd realize for himself."

Julie and I talked for hours in her tiny dorm room on the top floor of Baldwin House, which was equipped with a sturdy rope for an escape if necessary. I did not need to go beyond the editor's questions, but we kept talking, partly because I had hours until the next Peter Pan bus back to Cambridge and partly because we were comfortable talking. A more complicated and compelling picture of childhood in these two famous families began to form. For instance, we talked of their interaction with the Secret Service:

[David] told me that they were really like best friends. . . . There was always enough for a touch football game or something and that he just really liked them. In fact, he said, it was so sad when they left that he just went up to his room and didn't come down for a whole day and a whole night. They all said good-bye and he wouldn't come down from his room to say good-bye to them because he was so sad and he just couldn't.

I asked the editors at the *Ladies' Home Journal* if I could do a story that reached beyond the wedding. No, they wanted the story just as ordered. I said okay, but let me also do a second story for free. No, was the reply. In retrospect, the editors were right. All the magazine wanted to pay for was an innocuous story about a young couple in love. The story was published in August 1968 as "Again: Eisenhower and Nixon." Julie and David were married on December 22, at the Marble Collegiate Church in New York City.

The experience produced a story about the story in the *Harvard Summer News,* headlined "Nixon Biographer Writes about True Romance, Too." According to the paper, "Hess reports that he is not embarrassed, disgraced or ashamed to have this article published in a lady's magazine. He says if he wrote four articles a year for *Journal* he wouldn't have to work."

Miami Beach, 1968

Theodore White got it right: "No convention in history had been as dull as this except, perhaps, Eisenhower's renomination in San Francisco in 1956." This was August in South Florida. The temperature outside was 100° F. Inside the hotels spread along Collins Avenue, where candidates and state delegations made their headquarters, the air was set to chill a martini. We moved in and out, from freezing to boiling, in search of gossip or another camp follower. Soon our throats closed and were on fire.

Nixon Biographer Writes About True Romance, Too

By DEBORAH WAROFF

Richard Nixon's biographer, Stephen Hess, digressed recently from politics to love. He wrote a nice gooey article for the August **Ladies Home Journal** on "How Julie Nixon Fell in Love with David Eisenhower."

The story included all the details of their adolescent love, even the time Julie called Mother to ask advice because David came a callin' at Smith and she was washing her hair (for real, like with Shampoo) and she couldn't go downstairs to see him and she was afraid he would think she didn't want to see him. Mother told Julie to call David and tell all, and it worked out to a happily-ever-after.

Hess reports that he is not embarrassed, disgraced or ashamed to have this article published in a lady's magazine. He says if he wrote four articles a year for **Journal** he wouldn't have to work.

Right now Hess is a fellow of the Kennedy Institute, and has been working hard this year. His **Nixon, A Political Portrait**, written with Earl Mazo, fills the gap left between Mazo's 1959 biography and the present.

The biography was not authorized by Nixon, and Hess describes it as a "warts and all" version of the Nixon story. It recounts most of Nixon's dirty deeds and many of his others, while remaining sympathetic to the man.

When fresh out of grad school, Hess started as Eisenhower's number two speechwriter. He's been writing for and about Republicans ever since, and last year wrote **The Republican Establishment** with David Broder of the Washington Post.

When Hess get bored with straight politics he turns to political cartoons. A Hess book to be released in September, **The Ungentlemanly Art**, will be the first history of American political cartoonery. It covers funny pens from Ben Franklin to Thomas Nast to Herblock, and even uses political cartoons for footnotes.

My primary reason for being there was to promote the publication of *Nixon: A Political Portrait.* Writing a campaign biography is a long shot by definition. There is no reward for place or show; the win ticket, however, is bankable. In our case, there would be book contracts for scores of editions in exotic languages like Telugu, Odia, Kannada, and Malayalam, as well as something called "the ladder edition," a rewrite at content levels ranging from 1,000 to 5,000 words, primarily intended for young readers abroad for whom English is a second language. There was even to be a presentation edition for official use in Vietnam bound in elephant hide. Pirated copies were also produced in Hong Kong.

Our book was an unusual campaign biography in that reviewers did not treat it as political blather. Still, they brought along their own politics, meaning they tended to be either too flattering or not flattering enough. On this score, my favorite headline, from Eliot Fremont-Smith's review in the *New York Times,* was "All Warts and a Twinge of Sympathy."

And—important for sales—the book produced some news of its own. The first story was how Nixon, following secret phone calls from Mamie Eisenhower and Ike's doctor, turned down the Eisenhowers' offer to vigorously campaign for him in 1960. The *Chicago Tribune* devoted a 1,300-word editorial to "Nixon and Ike," in praise of Nixon's "act of self-sacrifice" and "his affectionate concern for Eisenhower's well-being." The second story was about co-author Earl Mazo's investigation of vote fraud in Chicago and Texas. In Texas, "a minimum of 100,000 votes officially tallied for the Kennedy-Johnson ticket simply were non-existent." The Democrats carried the state by 46,000 votes. His report on Chicago chicanery produced a long list of entries like the following: "Ward 6, Precinct 38: At about 10:15 A.M. the [voting machine] indicator indicated 121 votes [had been cast] after 43 persons had voted." Mazo was writing a twelve-part series in the *New York Herald Tribune,* but by mid-December 1960, after just four of the articles had appeared, Nixon asked to see him. "Right off, as we shook hands, he said, 'Earl, those are interesting articles you are writing—but no one steals the presidency of the United States.' I thought he might be kidding. But never was a man more deadly serious. Then, continent-by-continent, he enumerated potential international crises that could be dealt with only by the President of a united country." The *Herald Tribune,* as requested, stopped the series. Yet when the Mazo-Hess book was published, the July 28 headline in London's *Sunday Times* read, "Was Jack Kennedy's Election Rigged?"

The world of book promoting has its own vocabulary. The bookmaker is introduced to the green room, where guests wait to be interviewed on television. My first green room (which is rarely green) was on *Kup's Show,* in 1960. Irv Kupcinet, a popular columnist at the *Chicago Sun-Times,* hosted a Saturday night program that gathered an enormous variety of guests passing through the city. *Hats in the Ring,* being the first book by an unknown twenty-seven-year-old author, placed me in the last hour of the three-hour show. Waiting with me, the other third-hour guest was a twenty-two-year-old actress named Jane Fonda, who was plugging her first movie. *Tall Story* was about a young woman going to college to find a husband, preferably the basketball star played by Anthony Perkins. Fonda's publicist, I guess, had her dressed vamp style, in a slinky black low-cut dress with bouffant hair and heavy makeup, which was totally at odds with the character she played in the movie. I had the feeling she was not very happy about it. I tried hard not to ask her about Hollywood. Nor did she ask about the Eisenhower White House.

Promoting the *Nixon* book in Miami Beach had its own uniqueness. A Jewish restaurant at midmorning seemed like a strange place to do an interview. The unknown host was starting a career that would make him more famous than most of the authors he interviewed. Larry King never read your book, I learned, yet he listened—many hosts don't—and by the end of an interview you accepted that no one had understood your book better than he had.

On August 8, 1968, Richard Nixon accepted the Republican presidential nomination. It was the scenario he had laid out on September 27, 1961, in a Los Angeles press conference: He would be a candidate for governor of California in 1962 and not a candidate for president of the United States in 1964 (thus opting out of running during Kennedy's reelection year). Yet the road was not so easily mapped: along the way he lost in California, moved to New York (where he lacked a political base), never stopped campaigning for Republicans everywhere in 1964 and 1966, and was therefore appreciated by the most delegates in 1968.

The campaign would now start in earnest—but without me. I wished it were otherwise.

The 1968 Campaign and Spiro T. Agnew

There was one major surprise in Miami Beach. Spiro T. Agnew, governor of Maryland, was Nixon's choice for vice president.

Spiro *who*? The question echoed on the floor of the convention's last day. Agnew had been assigned to put Nixon's name in nomination, perhaps as a test. If so, he earned a C minus at best. His thirteen-minute speech, packed with clichés, was delivered in a monotone without any changes of inflection. Agnew had been governor for only two years, elected by accident in a Democratic state when the Democrats managed to nominate an outright racist, thus throwing the support of black voters to Agnew. After the rioting that followed the assassination of Martin Luther King Jr. in April 1968, Agnew summoned the state's black leaders to the capital and harshly attacked them for not controlling radicals. It was ugly. When Nixon chose a running mate in 1960, he thought of Henry Cabot Lodge as an asset. Maybe now there were no assets available. Nixon called together party leaders for advice, but it was an exercise in conservatives crossing out liberals like John Lindsay and liberals crossing out conservatives like Ronald Reagan. Nobody bothered to cross out Spiro Agnew. The Maryland governor had originally supported Nelson Rockefeller for the nomination, and his conversion must have added luster to Nixon's assessment of Agnew's judgment. So Nixon went forth with a vice-presidential candidate who lacked political experience beyond the tiny state of Maryland and had even less knowledge of national and international affairs.

Agnew would need help. When he met with Nixon's staff after the convention to go over the issues, the inside word was that he had failed the exam. John Sears, a young lawyer in Nixon's law firm who had proved his political smarts as a convention delegate-hunter, was assigned to the Agnew plane. In late August I received a frantic request: Would I travel with Agnew? Given the state of politics in Maryland, I first made a quick call to a friend at the *Wall Street Journal,* which I knew was investigating Agnew. They had no story. So I agreed to be at Baltimore's Friendship airport on September 17 as Agnew was beginning an eight-day swing through the West.

Before I could arrive, Agnew accused Democratic candidate Hubert Humphrey of being "squishy soft" on communism—an outrageous charge in light of Humphrey's long anti-communist record. Agnew was asked if he had been aware of the overtones of Joe McCarthy in what he was saying. "No, I was not," Agnew replied. "And of course I want to be completely candid. . . . Had I ever realized the effect that this expression would have, I would have shunned it like the plague." Agnew's statement is "incredible," according to veteran Washington journalist Jules Witcover: "The idea that a candidate for the Vice-Presidency of the United States could not have known the political history of 'soft on Communism' was incredible on the face of it. When Agnew used the phrase he was forty-nine years old; in the heyday of Joe McCarthy he was a practicing lawyer in his mid-thirties."

The gaffes did not stop. Two days later, on September 13, in Chicago, the press asked Agnew if he had any concern that there were so few Negroes in the crowds greeting him. "Very frankly, when I am moving in a crowd, I don't look and say, 'Well, there's a Negro, there's an Italian, and there's a Greek and there's a Polack. I'm just trying to meet the people and I'm glad that they're there and that they're friendly." His response inflamed Chicago's large Polish American community. That night at a large Republican reception, Agnew congratulated all the young people "in Illi-noise." His pronunciation was greeted with boos and catcalls.

When I arrived at the airport on September 17, reporters probably assumed I was responding to an SOS from Nixon headquarters. "Evidence that Richard M. Nixon is more disturbed by his running mate's open-mouthed campaign than he lets on is found in his discreet assignment of Stephen Hess, his longtime liberal advisor, to oversee Gov. Spiro T. Agnew." So wrote columnists Rowland Evans and Robert Novak in that morning's *Washington Post*. There was more: "The potential for disaster displayed by Agnew in just two weeks on the campaign trail has convinced Nixon he needs a trusted and cool head like Steve Hess's to represent his interests." I never found out where this story came from, but I knew it would complicate my life. The governor of Maryland, a man of pride and position, insecure and in over his head, was being told that someone he had probably never heard of was coming to pull him back from the brink.

Vice-presidential candidates are not expected to make much news. They go to less important places and repeat what their presidential candidates have already said. A reporter told me in 1964 that he had never had as much fun being on the plane of the losing vice-presidential candidate (William Miller, for trivia buffs) because it was so without consequences. Agnew, however, was not penciled in for losing. His gaffes gave reporters an attractive story that they would love to elevate to significant, which my appearance helped to confirm.

Their temptation was obvious from the coverage of the first speech I wrote for Agnew. After the Texas Republican convention in Fort Worth, the headline in the *New York Times* was "Agnew Declares Peace Is Top Aim." That was perfect—it was not a speech designed to make news. But reporter Homer Bigart insisted on seeing a story behind the speech: "Mr. Agnew, who prefers speaking off-the-cuff, used a prepared text. His speech was peppered with light banter aimed at Vice President Humphrey. This sprightliness may indicate the influence of Stephen Hess, a speech writer for former President Dwight D. Eisenhower and Mr. Nixon who joined the Agnew party last week." In the *Washington Post,* Richard Homan also wanted readers to know there was something noteworthy going on within the Agnew campaign. The speech "sparkled with new wit and bristled with new gibes—most delivered with poor timing in a monotone that almost flattened the previously bubbling audience."

Could I get the reporters back on track? Probably not, but I tried. In an interview with the *Baltimore Evening Sun*, "Mr. Hess said he has a 'passion for anonymity. . . . I'll never take credit for any line. . . . I'm sorry there's as much stir about my being aboard as there is.' . . . Mr. Hess says the timing of his arrival was 'absolute coincidence' and takes no credit for any changes that have been wrought in Mr. Agnew."

Before I joined Agnew, someone wrote a speech for him titled "Reducing Population Density." I do not know who wrote it or how it came to him. The speech had an attractive visionary ring that was not evident in anything else about Agnew. The thesis was that there must be ways to reduce overcrowding in our cities, "the impaction that breeds despair." The text then called for "the establishment of new towns." We were flying from Dallas to Cheyenne. The area in the Agnew plane behind the cockpit served as the candidate's quarters, then a section for staff, the remainder for use by reporters. I moved up to sit next to Agnew. It was night; barely a twinkle of light could be seen on the ground. A few lights over there, a few more lights someplace else. "Governor, perhaps Wyoming is not the right place for the population speech." He nodded.

Being visited by the next vice president of the United States must be a pretty big event in Cheyenne, Wyoming. The cheers, the costumes, the music are what campaigns are supposed to be all about.

Then Agnew delivered "Reducing Population Density." Was there a collective gasp from the audience or was that my imagination?

I went back to the hotel wondering what to make of what I had just seen. Could he not have understood what "relieving population crowding" might mean to people living in the state with the lowest population density of the lower forty-eight? Eventually there was a knock on my door. Agnew's aide, Art Sohmer, told me the governor would like to see me. I found a dejected Agnew, seated in his suite's one comfortable chair, with papers spread over the floor. He looked up: "Steve, I picked up the wrong speech."

I said nothing. I felt sorry for him. But his job was to speak words that are helpful to the presidential candidate. My job was to provide him with appropriate words, some serious, some amusing, raising the level of discourse if possible. The moment he picked up the wrong speech at the wrong time seemed to break any connection there was between us, and afterward he went back to off-the-cuff speaking, which was apparently more comfortable than reading someone else's words. I continued drafting statements in his name, such as "Toward a More Perfect Union," with four related position papers that dealt with the problems of federalism. He initialed them, but they were not noticed. Why report on them, reporters told me, when they were not delivered by the candidate himself? (A perfectly good question.) I was not going to quit, and he could not fire me. So we traveled on—civilly, without anger.

After Cheyenne we turned south for Las Vegas, where the reporters and some of the staff stayed up late talking and gambling. One of the reporters was Gene Oishi of the *Baltimore Sun*. The next morning Oishi—a Japanese American who, as a child, had been sent with his family to the Japanese internment camp in Tule Lake, California—was dozing in the plane's press section when Agnew spied him. "What's the matter with the fat Jap?" As a purely political crisis, "fat Jap" beat "Polack" in the sense that Agnew was soon heading to Hawaii, a state with a substantial number of Japanese American voters. Agnew's response was to play the Greek card. "It is rather ridiculous [to charge] the son of a Greek immigrant [with] insensitivity to the national pride and heritage of other peoples." The problem, he said, was that he had "inadvertently" used two slurs in less than a week.

At this point, the *Washington Post* had heard enough. In a long, bold-headlined editorial, "The Perils of Spiro," readers were told that naming "Agnew as [Nixon's] running mate may come to be regarded as perhaps the most eccentric political appointment since the Roman emperor Caligula named his horse a consul." After presenting evidence, the editorial concluded by saying that "for the moment, our sympathies are with Stephen Hess and John Sears, the two very able men Nixon has dispatched to keep an eye on the Governor. The specter of Spiro leaping from crag to crag with the press in hot pursuit is a beguiling one. . . . You can view Agnew with alarm; or you can point to him with pride, but for now we prefer to look on with horrified fascination. What will he do next? What will he say?"

The best way to limit harm, it appeared, was to limit Agnew, whose schedule was henceforth severely reduced. The governor seemed delighted to be doing less campaigning. James Perry, reporting for the *National Observer,* shadowed Agnew for three days (he also spent three days following Democratic vice-presidential candidate Edmund Muskie):

> I joined Mr. Agnew in Milwaukee on Sunday. On Sunday, Mr. Agnew rested. On Monday, we departed the Pfister Hotel at 8:30 a.m. and arrived in Toledo at 11:05 a.m. Mr. Agnew gave a speech in Toledo at 11:05. Mr. Agnew gave a speech at Levis Square and then retired to the Commodore Perry Hotel for "staff time" in his suite. At 3:45 p.m. he taped a short and inconsequential television interview at WTOL-TV. We left Toledo at 5:30 p.m. CDT. Mr. Agnew retired to his suite at the O'Hare Inn for further "staff time." Thereafter, he retired for the night.
>
> In three days, then, Mr. Agnew made two speeches, two television tapings, and one appearance at a fund-raising dinner. In contrast, Sen. Edmund S. Muskie, the Democratic candidate for Vice President, came to Chicago on Wednesday and spoke at seven rallies, taped two television shows, and squeezed in a private meeting with the editors of the *Chicago Sun-Times.*

The campaign tour inched forward. Agnew made one last gaffe. In response to a reporter's question on why he was not spending time in America's cities, part of his response was, "If you've seen one city slum, you've seen them all." Pat Buchanan joined us for a week. "Agnew and I got on famously and would forever remain friends," he would later write. On election night I went to the Governor's Mansion in Annapolis to say good-bye to my traveling companions of 60,000 miles and then caught a plane to New York City to celebrate Nixon's becoming president-elect in the morning. As for Agnew, his behavior as vice president was in keeping with his misperformance as a candidate. Buchanan and I would disagree, of course. Yet these facts are not in dispute: Agnew was convicted in federal court of failing to report $29,500 in taxable income in a scheme with Maryland contractors that netted roughly $100,000. He was sentenced to three years' probation and fined $10,000. On October 10, 1973, in a letter to Secretary of State Henry Kissinger, Agnew resigned from "the Office of Vice President of the United States effective immediately."

Deputy Assistant to the President for Urban Affairs

I had paid my dues to the campaign, and it was now time to consider what I would like my reward to be. I knew what I did not want: I did not want to go back to the White House. I had been there—it had been wonderful—but now I wanted to move on. The Nixon transition headquarters was in the Hotel Pierre on New York's Fifth Avenue. Bryce Harlow, from an office next to the president-elect, sent me a note saying he was going to find the right job for me. It was a long November, waiting. Then, as expected, the unexpected.

Pat Moynihan, my liberal Democratic friend, called from Cambridge. The president-elect wanted to see him. They had never met. *The Professor and the President: Daniel Patrick Moynihan in the Nixon White House,* my 2015 book, begins, "I am the only person—perhaps in the world—who was a friend of both Richard Nixon and Daniel Patrick Moynihan before they knew each other." Was I to be a bridge of sorts? Pat asked me to meet him at the Pierre.

After his session with Nixon, Pat bounded into the hotel's dining room, exploding with excitement and first impressions. He had been offered a new position that sounded like the urban equivalent of Henry Kissinger running the National Security Council. It was Pat's dream job, if not his dream president. We drank a bottle of good Beaujolais, more than I was accustomed to. Pat could not get over Nixon admitting how little he knew about the domestic policies of his country. "He's ignorant!" Pat almost shouted. "He doesn't know anything—I would have

*Moynihan and Hess on the South Lawn of the White House after
President Clinton announces the nomination of Ruth Bader Ginsburg.*

bluffed it." Pat told me he had already decided to accept the president-elect's offer, and urged me to join him in the White House. He talked about what a great team we would make. Of course I would go.

I had two reasons for accepting.

First, I could not imagine having more fun in government than with Pat Moynihan. Pat's life, for those who were willing to share it, was an adventure of walking ideas across a high wire, a bit dangerous, full of the unplanned. Even his transition to the White House started with an exclamation point. Averell Harriman lent him his Georgetown mansion, complete with wine cellar. (Pat had been Harriman's assistant when Harriman was governor of New York.) Did the other incoming staffers dine on fine china, surrounded by the impressionist paintings of Cezanne and Van Gogh?

Second, Pat needed me! He was about to work for a president he had vigorously opposed in the recent campaign, alongside registered Republicans of whom he may never have known more than one (me). In baseball terms, I saw myself as his bench coach, the person sitting next to the manager to offer strategic advice. What did it mean, for example, when Nixon referred to himself as a moderate? His moderation was not the usual kind, walking a path down the middle of the political spectrum, looking to balance each proposal. Rather, Nixon's moderation was arrived at by averaging. High minus low equals moderate. Pat would have to keep this in mind. Say Nixon accepted a conservative proposal, such as appointing a conservative to the Supreme Court: that would then be an opportune time for Pat to push a liberal proposal. This was moderation in the Nixonian calculation: high minus low equals moderate.

Pat commandeered two large offices for us in the West Wing, on the ground floor. After the inaugural parade moved down Pennsylvania Avenue, I took my sons into the White House to see my new office. Jamie Hess, a few days past his fifth birthday, looked the place over and concluded, "Not bad, Daddy, not bad." The National Gallery of Art and the Smithsonian lent us paintings for our bare walls. Pat picked a massive self-portrait of cartoonist Thomas Nast, famous for fighting Tammany Hall corruption. I borrowed paintings by African American artists: a small Jacob Lawrence and a large canvas by the wonderful Washington colorist Alma Thomas, whose work forty years later would again adorn the walls of the White House, this time chosen by First Lady Michelle Obama.

Our windows looked out on Lafayette Square. One day I saw that overnight the park had been enclosed by a high wooden fence. I called upstairs to White House Counsel John Ehrlichman.

"John, there is an unpainted fence around Lafayette Square."

"So?" Ehrlichman replied.

"When the President wakes up tomorrow and looks out the window, what do you think he will see spelled out in large letters on that fence?"

John got it. "What should we do?" he asked.

"You get paint, I'll get the schoolchildren of the District of Columbia to paint patriotic murals."

And so an exciting depiction of American history through the eyes of predominantly black youngsters went up across from the White House. The Smithsonian will ask if the national collection can have the murals. Too late. The fence was junked immediately after construction.

A White House aide should always be on the lookout for unpainted fences, but if I had a formal job description it would have been something like this: the deputy assistant to the president for urban affairs in the office of Daniel Patrick Moynihan was responsible for trying to maintain enough order so that the staff would know—at the same time, if possible—what Pat was asking each of us to do. We worked very hard, six-day workweeks, as many hours a day as possible, with heavy lifting by four incredibly smart and dedicated young men: Richard Blumenthal and Christopher DeMuth (both twenty-two years old), Chester "Checker" Finn (twenty-five), and John Price (thirty). When others were added— White House Fellows, interns, detailees from the civil service, academics on brief assignments—we transformed into a flock of brilliantly plumed, rapidly moving hummingbirds. At thirty-five, I was the old man.

Each assistant had an area of expertise—education, the environment, the District of Columbia, poverty programs. My area of expertise was Daniel Patrick Moynihan: what he needed, when, and how to get it.

During the administration's first week, Pat proposed to the president that a vest-pocket park be built on the site of four buildings that had burned down during the race riots of the previous April. Nixon loved the idea—cheap yet symbolic. A date was picked for the president to be there, January 31. The tight schedule would permit no setbacks. Then the guard at the Northwest Gate called to say that a Mr. Cohen wanted to see Dr. Moynihan. I knew who he was, and instructed the guard to direct him to my office. Mr. Cohen and his brother owned one of the four buildings. He told me that when the rioters destroyed their store, the police ordered them to clean up the mess at their own expense or be fined. He was very upset, and he was eager to tell the public how they had been mistreated. I sympathized, and told him I was very sorry the president was not around to see him. I took him on a quick tour of the West Wing so he could see that the president was not in his office. Mr. Cohen was now more collected. But it was after five o'clock and he said he had missed his bus. I ordered a White House car to take him home, a black Mercury with a uniformed military driver. This was the least I could do. Later, the motor pool told me that when Mr. Cohen got home he told the driver to wait so that his wife and children could get in and drive around the neighborhood. All so President Nixon, in his second week in office, could pose in front of a gutted Waxie Maxie's record store on 7th Street in Northwest D.C.

Another example: Bud Wilkinson, the great University of Oklahoma football coach, was a consultant to the administration charged with voluntary sector interests. Pat was irritated that Wilkinson had brought a group of college athletic directors to the White House and blindsided the president by asking that their football fields (idle in the summer) be used for youth poverty programs. Pat came into my office—he did not sit down—to tell me that the president wanted this done and that I should work out the details. The program wasn't bad, it just wasn't good. The athletic fields were in the wrong places, not located where the young people lived, nor was there any educational element. And, of course, the program would take limited funds away from better programs. I negotiated a contract for less than the coaches wanted. While I did not save the taxpayer a great deal of money, I still felt I had done some good.

Pat had told me it was important for Nixon's consumer affairs advisers, Virginia Knauer and Liddy Hanford, to get to know Ralph Nader. Call him, he said. Assuming the flame-throwing liberal could be lured by my invitation to lunch at the White House, I made the arrangements. Then, forgetting the date, I had already eaten lunch when he arrived. So I ate a second lunch as Virginia, Liddy, and Ralph got to know each other. Liddy Hanford would go on to become Senator Elizabeth Dole from the state of North Carolina—one of four members of Nixon's 1969 staff who became senators. Moynihan, Lamar Alexander, and Richard Blumenthal were the other three.

Pat promised the Massachusetts AFL-CIO he would give the keynote address at its annual convention. When something more immediately important came up, I grabbed his speech and got on a plane for Boston. What was quickly obvious was that the restless unionists were not interested in a forty-five-minute lecture on national urban policy. So instead, they got fifteen minutes of Moynihan stories and a few jokes, for which I was politely applauded for being so brief. Other last-minute Hess-for-Moynihan switches took me to conferences in Hong Kong and Singapore, where my reading of Pat's lecture on U.S. national urban policy was more appreciated.

Some assignments had more consequences. The summer of 1968 had seen an upheaval in black communities across the country. Would 1969 be equally explosive? If so, the government would have to invest in cooling-off programs. I was to investigate and come back with a prediction. Among the places I visited was the FBI, the only time I have ever been there. Their civil rights files were worthless for my predictive purposes, even the newspaper clippings labeled confidential. The riots of 1968 had taken the heaviest toll predominantly on the very places black people lived. My guess was they would not want this to happen again, and therefore 1969 would not be a repeat of 1968. Thankfully, this turned out to be correct.

Domestic policymaking during Nixon's first year in office instantly became more complicated than Pat had bargained for when he accepted the job—"instantly" meaning day three, January 23, when the White

House issued the following statement from the president: "Today I am pleased to announce Dr. Arthur Burns, a longtime friend and trusted adviser, has agreed to join the White House staff as the Counsellor to the President. Dr. Burns will have Cabinet rank. He will head up a small group whose prime responsibility will be the coordination of the development of my domestic policies and programs." In short, Nixon was giving essentially the same job to Dr. Burns that he had already given to Dr. Moynihan. Moreover, as I wrote in *The Professor and the President*, "In the White House version of the rock-paper-scissors game, virtually all the advantages appear to be with Burns: Burns's cabinet rank covers Moynihan's position of senior staff. Burns's 'domestic affairs' mandate covers Moynihan's 'urban affairs.' Burns is a Republican and an old friend of the president; Moynihan is neither. Burns is conservative; Moynihan liberal (and Nixon is more conservative than liberal)."

The struggles between the two famous Ivy League combatants, Moynihan of Harvard and Burns of Columbia, were largely over a welfare proposal called the Family Assistance Plan. It was at the heart of what the liberal Moynihan wanted government to do but was way too expensive for the conservative Burns. The resolution came when the president addressed the nation on August 8—and the surprise was that Moynihan won.

With the speech putting the pieces of domestic policy in place, the White House staff would be reorganized. John Ehrlichman would replace both Burns and Moynihan in a "position [that] will be roughly equivalent in domestic matters to the position held by Dr. Henry Kissinger in national security affairs." Dr. Burns was nominated to be the next chairman of the Federal Reserve. Dr. Moynihan would become counselor to the president, with cabinet rank, without specific responsibilities. Pat was pleased by this change. He never lacked for things he wanted to do, especially from a White House address, and he would be returning to Harvard in a year. His young assistants would, for the most part, stay with Ehrlichman for a short time and then move on to law school or take off to travel around the world. This left only one other personnel question: What did they want to do with me?

To HEW

As I walked into the Oval Office, I looked forward to being surprised. What was the man behind the Wilson desk going to say? I would like to stay in government, which he knew, but I had not asked for anything. I also knew there was no room for me on the revised White House staff that Chief of Staff Bob Haldeman was designing.

What the president said, in effect, was that Bob Finch was failing as secretary of health, education and welfare. He spoke in sorrow, a tone I had never heard in his voice before. Bob was the only person in Nixon's cabinet he really cared about, his campaign manager when he ran for the presidency in 1960, the person he would have liked to have picked as his running mate in 1968. Nixon also implied that he did not think much of Finch's deputy secretary, Jack Veneman.

My instructions were to go over to HEW and see if I could straighten things out. "Yes, Mr. President," I said, as I walked out the door. But I was thinking, "How the hell am I going to do that?" The job was awful enough even absent any guidance from Nixon on how this might be accomplished.

Bob and Jack were my friends, and I liked them very much. We agreed with each other more than we did with most others in the administration. It was clear that I could not just walk in and say, "The president thinks you've failed." What I could say was, "Can I be helpful?" Perhaps hint at a little more. More than that would have been an embarrassment to the three of us (especially as it would have been leaked to the press). They were smart politicians: they knew why I was there and probably why he had sent me.

Finch and Veneman had to find something for me to do. The something was called the White House Conference on Children and Youth, started by Theodore Roosevelt in 1909, held once every tenth year, and already a year behind schedule. The president had not even appointed a national chairman. Would I be interested? It was not an attractive prospect, but they assured me it would only be for a year.

The administration had just closed its first White House conference on December 4, 1969—the White House Conference on Food, Nutrition and Health, better known as the White House Conference on Hunger. I met with its chairman, Harvard professor Jean Mayer, whose words of wisdom were that he should have held the conference on an aircraft carrier so he could have thrown the troublemakers overboard! I was not supposed to laugh. The mass-attended White House conference format, he told me, is a recipe for disaster in this age of overlapping conflicts. Bring together enough people in a prominent site, mix in the media, and you will see.

On December 5, 1969, President Nixon announced that Stephen Hess was leaving his staff to become national chairman of the White House Conference on Children and Youth: "The White House Conference can and will define problems, seek new knowledge, evaluate past success and failure, and outline alternative courses of action."

In less than a month, I came to the realization that a conference combining issues of children and youth was not going to work. The needs and problems of children and young people were then, as they are now, profoundly different. My most immediate concern was that the voice of young people protesting Vietnam would completely overwhelm everything else. These voices deserved to be heard, but a White House conference was not a logical place. Rather, it would only drown out debate on what government should be doing in the children's field.

I headed back to the White House to ask the president for permission to divide the conference down the middle. He agreed. There would be a White House Conference on Children in December 1970 and a White House Conference on Youth in April 1971.

My job would be for only two years.

The White House Conference on Children

There are so many firsts for a manager who has never managed before. The first of the firsts had to be to find money, some from private contributions, most from the federal government. The experts at HEW helped me prepare a budget that I took before the Subcommittee on Labor, Health, Education and Welfare of the House Appropriations Committee. They warned me that the chairman of the subcommittee was the most terrifying of all those from whom they sought funds—Representative Daniel Flood, Democrat from Pennsylvania, whose pointed, waxed mustache made him look like the villain in a silent movie.

Chairman Flood opened the hearing, speaking in his dramatic, clipped accent. His question went on and on and on. Finally, he seemed to be waiting for my answer.

"Mr. Chairman, I am sorry. I do not understand your question."

"Neither do I!" His laugh caused an uproar.

The question must have meant something to somebody. But an unknowing answer would have brought doom down upon me. Instead, my retreat ended up getting me the money I needed.

At the time, I thought this was the end of the story. But several weeks later two strangers showed up to announce that they were going to produce brochures and other public relations materials for the conference in return for the $100,000 from my budget they were promised. How should I get rid of them? I decided to wait them out. They kept coming back, but, like Penelope waiting out her suitors, I was never quite ready to sign a contract. Finally they stopped coming. Chairman Flood, however, apparently continued his stratagems with other parties. Eventually he was censured by Congress, resigned in disgrace, and pled guilty in federal court to accepting payoffs.

Clearly, I was entering a dangerous universe beyond the semi-anonymity of the White House staff. I had known a dash of unpleasant publicity during the presidential campaign, but that was really directed at Agnew. Now I had to be aware that my job could attract ill news. Here is a small example, though not so small to a young man named Jim Rosapepe. Rosapepe, whom I had made an unpaid intern, had attracted the attention of muckraker columnist Jack Anderson. Under the *Washington Post* headline "Nixon's Unwanted Militant," Anderson wrote that Jim was supposedly a "radical liberal" who had "rubbed some of his elders the wrong way" as president of a youth council in Arlington, Virginia. "Hess has refused to fire the young activist." (Jim would one day be appointed U.S. ambassador to Romania.) This was the same principle I exercised when I rejected White House counsel John Dean's request to fire a Youth Conference delegate. Was I just too stiff-necked in this get-along Washington? After two tours in the White House, I asked my cousin Carole, whose opinion I valued, why no one ever offered me anything that I knew better than to accept? She replied that it is because they knew I would not accept. Maybe it was that simple.

A pet peeve of mine had always been government's capacity to make things ugly. Now I had a budget and the right to worry about the appearance of whatever the White House Conference on Children was going to produce—posters, reports, stationery, binders, badges, whatnot. I hired the noted graphic designer Ivan Chermayeff, whose sleek, modernist art featured bold primary colors. Suddenly everything was bright red flowers with fat green leaves, seemingly painted by a small child, which the *Washington Post* described as a "touching connotation of frailty, hope and joy." The *Post* published an editorial hoping that my campaign to improve government graphics could set an example.

Again, there was more to the story. Some in the social work establishment were outraged that I was spending money on art design that could instead be spent on antipoverty programs. They did not want to be convinced that good design does not cost more than the usual drab stuff. Yet their criticism did cause me to reconsider (somewhat): I was being paid to run a conference, not seek good art. So the design for the Youth Conference had to measurably tone down the visual acuity.

The White House Conference on Children began on the evening of December 13 at Washington's Sheraton-Park Hotel with an opening address by the president of the United States. As the conference's national chairman, I was on the platform with him. While I had written a lot of words for Richard Nixon, I had never heard anything like his remarks that night. I found out later that the president couldn't sleep, and at 4:30 a.m. he began to rewrite:

I remember back in the Depression years . . . how deeply I felt about the plight of those people my own age who used to come into my father's store when they couldn't pay the bill, because their fathers were out of work, and how this seemed to separate them from others in our school. None of us had any money in those days, but those in families where there were no jobs and there was nothing but the little that relief then offered suffered from more than simply going without. What they suffered was a hurt to their pride that many carried with them for the rest of their lives.

Early the next morning, deep in sleep, a ringing phone: "The President is calling."

"Steve, why isn't my speech on the front page in the *Times*?"

"I haven't yet seen the *Times*, Mr. President. What's the byline?"

He told me it was a UPI piece.

"That explains it," I say. "The *Times* reporter should have been Nan Robertson, but her husband is very ill in the hospital. The *Times* isn't going to lead the paper with a wire service story."

This satisfied him.

"How was the *Post*?" I asked.

"Okay," he said and hung up.

Poor Nixon, the UPI story that the *Times* ran on page 19 is a hack piece. The *Post* article that failed to interest the president is on the front page, well written, with a three-column photograph captioned "President Nixon and Mayor (Walter) Washington shake hands in greeting at children's conference." To be accurate, there were three people in that photograph. The unidentified person in the middle between the president and the mayor was me. Perhaps this was the ultimate definition of a bit player.

Involving more than 100 staff members, with 4,000 delegates filling three major Washington hotels, the White House Conference on Children fit inside a $3.2 million budget. In contrast to the endless sessions of long-winded delegates reading technical papers and prepackaged reso-

shington Post

Times Herald

MAY, DECEMBER 14, 1970

Phone 223-6000   Circulation 223-6100   Classified 223-6200

Index

Amusements	C 8
Classified	C12
City Life	B 1
Comics	C 7
Crossword	B 8
Editorials	A22

JFK

n crisis and his
ppraisals of Presi-
nhower, Kennedy
of Fidel Castro
talin's daughter,
lliluyeva.

of Missiles

ev reveals that
ought of putting
issiles in Cuba
was visiting Bul-
y, 1962. His justi-
s to prevent the
tes from launch-
calls "the inevit-
d invasion" in
ro surely "would

to think up some
fronting America
than words. But
ly? The logical
s missiles," he
ys he and other
ers first heard on
f the Bay of Pigs
e previous year.
ev's idea was to
ssiles into Cuba
tting the United
out until it was
o anything about
the result was
of perilous ten-
ich "the Ameri-
rying to frighten
y were no less
n we were of

er Soviet leader
esponsibility for

By Matthew Lewis—The Washington Post

President Nixon and Mayor Washington shake hands in greeting at children's conference.

President Asks Passage Now
Of Family Income Floor Plan

By Morton Mintz

The President recalled the ter than what we have

Bon
Dov
In

Seco
Shot
In Ca

Communi
shot down
with top-se
equipment
F-100 fight
a key batt
bodia, the
reported ye

The annou
Air Force
ground fire
over the Ho
southern La
ants said th
lieves the ai
tection equi
stroyed and
North Vietna
two-man crew

The F-100
apparently w
port mission
forces under
Communists
Cham Pro
Phnom Penh
pilot was pic
the U.S. Com

U.S. offici

lutions (the 1960 conference passed over 650), I was determined to give the participants something stimulating and, yes, fun. I even set up an Office of Special Events charged with making the gathering as untraditional as possible. At one of our forums, "Children Without Prejudice," an elementary school teacher from Iowa segregated her committee members by eye color, providing "the blue-eyed people" with humiliating experiences and "the brown-eyed people" with preferential treatment. Other groups filmed conditions at Washington's Junior Village and visited local schools and hospitals. The delegates exploring "Expressions of Identity: The School-Age Child" turned their meeting room into an "environment" that simulated as nearly as possible the manner in which a child's identity is formed. We even put on a show of music and dance, "The Sounds of Children," directed by Marge Champion, and including choreography by the magnificent Katherine Dunham.

I paid a price for this direction. The old-line establishment organizations that ran the 1960 conference—and wanted to run the 1970 conference—went into "unofficial" meetings to try to force me to hold a massive plenary session that would result in a blizzard of 1960-type resolutions. This was a fight over process, not substance, and it was catnip to the reporters. My objective was to conclude the conference with a tightly written set of goals that could be taken to the president, Congress, and state legislatures. The opposition's strategy was to defeat me by uniting with the conference's black caucus and other minority groups, which might be difficult for me to oppose. However, my friend Charles Hurst, the president of Malcolm X College in Chicago, was the dominant voice among blacks at the conference. He told me what he wanted, and I told him what I could give him. We came to an agreement. When the meeting to oppose my plan opened with remarks by a white woman, he jumped up to declare it "the greatest insult." The *Post* reported that the opposition "disintegrated."

The next day the White House Conference on Children ended. The delegates ranked sixteen "overriding concerns" in order of importance and assigned "highest priority" to six recommendations for remedial action. I announced that the six-day meeting was "an unqualified success," and Dr. Hurst called it "the most successful conference" in the sixty-one-year history of such meetings and praised its chairman as a man of "certified integrity" and fairness.

The ultimate question, however, as phrased by Gilbert Steiner, the leading scholar in the field, was whether "the White House conference is a better technique for bolstering the ego of many of its participants than for formulating a workable policy program." The answer, presumably, was very clear to him.

A White House Conference on Youth

On November 15, 1969, 300,000 protesters crowded into Washington, about 40,000 of whom circled the White House in a silent "march of death," carrying placards bearing the names of Americans killed in Vietnam. On the National Mall, Pete Seeger sang John Lennon's new song, "Give Peace a Chance." Thousands took up the song as Seeger shouted, "Are you listening, Nixon?" The antiwar movement was more than a youth crusade, yet 40,000 mostly young men had died in Vietnam by the end of 1968, nearly 12,000 more died in 1969, and 434,000 troops were still there.

"Asking this Administration to hold a conference on youth," said one long-time Republican official, "is like asking the Kremlin to hold a conference on capitalism." This was written in a *Washington Post Magazine* profile titled "Stephen Hess' Impossible Mission at the White House."

I was not naïve. I had been speaking on college campuses because someone from Washington had to go. The students kept telling me that these were the worst of times, and I gained no traction by telling them what it might have been like growing up in 1859 or 1929. I remember one painful appearance at the College of Wooster in Ohio, where an especially abusive student kept shouting at me. As I was waiting in the green room to leave, she came to apologize for her language. We talked. Where was she from? Arlington, Virginia. Her father worked for the CIA.

When I presented my youth conference plan at the White House, Bob Haldeman was at one end of the table, John Ehrlichman at the other. I was caught in a withering crossfire perhaps having more to do with their college-age children than with me. I left to fly to Salt Lake City, where I was trying to raise money for the conference. On arrival, a state trooper told me that the White House was calling. It was Bob Finch, who by then had been moved to the White House. He was disturbed by my treatment at the Haldeman-Ehrlichman meeting and offered me an ambassadorship to the UN in New York. I thanked him but explained that I had to see this through.

Now the good news: the White House Conference on Youth was not a disaster!

First, who were the delegates?

Nixon, as heard on a White House tape recording, asked Haldeman: "Did we have people from Texas A&M there, for example?"

> Haldeman: "I'm sure there was somebody but we, the people that were there were—"
> Nixon: "Mainly Harvard, Yale, and Stanford."
> Haldeman: "All over. Little bit of everything, but they're inevitably activist types."
> Nixon: "I see, I guess there wasn't much we could do about it."

Haldeman was right: The delegates were activists in their communities. And Nixon was wrong: this was not a Harvard-Yale-Stanford gathering.

We tried to match the demographics of the youth population—by geography, race, sex, age, current status (in school or working or unemployed)—and came close to meeting our goals. There were some misses: we had 5 percent fewer working youth, 3 percent fewer females. But high school students were 38.8 percent, the exact percentage of the population. We slightly overinvited minorities on purpose, otherwise there would have been too few to be on all the committees.

During the summer of 1970 the staff, led by my deputy Stephen Danzansky, put together a 120-member advisory task force that met in late August on the Irvine campus of the University of California to define the scope and character of the conference and to develop a plan of operations. They gave me three pieces of advice that truly shaped the conference's success. The first, already mentioned, was that the demographic composition should reflect the true range of young people. Second, they wanted the conference to meet with "the adults who count," not just other young people. As a result, we designed the conference to consist of a thousand youth and 500 adults, ultimately including ten members of Congress, fourteen presidents of colleges or universities, eight judges, and seven mayors. Third, they wanted the conference to be held outside Washington but not on a college campus, to underscore that it was to be a youth conference rather than a student conference. They liked the idea of a semiremote setting, partly so that the adult delegates would not be distracted by other commitments.

After my experience with the children's conference, I was delighted to be offered a format that might minimize the type of Washington-based delegate-media interaction in which conflict blankets substance. The youth conference site was to be a YMCA camping center near Estes Park, Colorado, on the eastern slope of the Continental Divide. While there were probably over a hundred journalists there, including all the TV networks, their reporting did not cycle back to the conference site (except through the *Rocky Mountain News,* the only newspaper available). This meant that the delegates were not reacting to news accounts—sometimes negative—as had the delegates at the children's conference.

The conference kicked off with a general meeting on April 18, 1971. As I began my greeting, several young men in work shirts and jeans rushed the stage and tried to pull the microphone from me. I asked them for a chance to finish my remarks. Then I turned the rostrum over to the dissidents. They announced a proposal to manage the conference. I immediately called for a vote and the delegates shouted them down with a resounding no. The radicals disappeared. I then introduced Elliot Richardson, Bob Finch's replacement as HEW secretary, who formally pledged the president's interest in their deliberations.

The staff had worked hard to find a beautiful locale high in the Rockies, 8,000 feet above sea level, five miles from the resort town of Estes Park, sixty miles from Denver. They checked the weather history and reported no problem. But when the delegates woke up the next morning, they were in the eye of a driving snowstorm that would eventually pile up to two feet. This was the dramatic picture that made news around the world. My remarkable staff rushed out to buy every available green plastic Glad Bag to encase the delegates' feet. Soon the army base at nearby Fort Carson provided us with parkas and boots, and the delegates got down to work in ten issue areas.

I appointed a task force to write a preamble to what would be the White House Youth Conference Report, which was read to the delegates by Karen Rux of Durham, North Carolina, with rafter-shaking gusto:

To the people:
    We are in the midst of a political, social and cultural revolution. Uncontrolled technology and the exploitation of people by people threaten to dehumanize our society. We must reaffirm the recognition of life as the supreme value which will not bear manipulation for other ends.

This stunning table-setter was received with thunderous applause and prairie whoops. Then the delegates voted for a long list of resolutions, including a complete withdrawal from Vietnam by December 31, the end of the draft and the creation of an all-volunteer army, legalization of marijuana under government auspices, tolerance of "any sexual behavior" between consenting individuals, an adequate income guaranteed for all, adoption of the Equal Rights Amendment, support for the eighteen-year-old vote, and the resignation of FBI director J. Edgar Hoover. Strangely, perhaps, the delegates chose not to directly attack the president.

Because of the media warp, we would not know how the conference was received beyond our encampment until we came down from the mountain. It was like waiting for the next morning's reviews after opening night on Broadway.

Roger Rapoport wrote in *Rolling Stone* of the heavy hand of Hess . . . chicanery by the Hess organization . . . bad housing . . . dreadful evening meals . . . dope smoking . . . and scenes like "an elderly professor slid his left arm around the back of the young blonde girl beside him and began groping for her left breast."

None of the major publications—*Time, Newsweek, New York Times*—shared Rapoport's disdain. The *Saturday Review* was the most enthusiastic: "The young people had found their voice. They were no longer isolated individuals separated by distrust and futility." Flora Lewis, the great foreign correspondent who was then writing a national column, graciously wrote that "Hess had a monumental job to do in the most trying circumstances. . . . He won't get much gratitude from his chief or his young guests. . . . But he's an honest man." After reading John Mathews in *The Nation,* my communications director, Mary Nell York, sent me the following note, "Steve, Did you see this? If this is the worst John can say, then the Conference was even more successful than I thought."

It would be many years before I learned what my chief thought. In 2013, I asked my friend Luke Nichter, the professor who had unraveled Nixon's White House tapes, if he could find any references to my running the youth conference. He said he'd try, "as long as you have thick skin." This is what he found:

Track 1, April 22, 1971

Nixon: I wonder if you have been in touch with that youth conference out there? I talked to a congressman who had been out there. . . . He said it was about 90 percent socialist left-wing Eastern liberal. . . .

Haldeman: Ah well, his percentages are wrong, but his—

Nixon: He said they adopted a resolution to abolish the capitalist system. . . .

Haldeman: I don't think that's right.

Nixon: Oh, I know he is right on that because I saw it. He showed it to me.

Haldeman: I don't think Steve was a good idea. . . . It wasn't a very good idea in terms of control of the conference because Steve just isn't that kind of—

Nixon: Oh, no, I know. . . . But this is enough of Hess now, just don't promise him anything more. Have we promised him anything more?

Haldeman: I certainly hope not, not to my knowledge.

Nixon: Well, I'm not promising him anything more. . . . Let him go out and yack.

Haldeman: Write a book or something.

Nixon: Huh? Write his book. It's not that he's at fault, but Steve leans in that direction. . . .

Haldeman: He's tried hard. He really has.

Nixon: Maybe he does.

Haldeman: He's always going to be going in the wrong direction.

Nixon: Um-hm.

Track 2, April 27, 1971 (with Haldeman)

Nixon: I've been too rough on Hess.

Track 3, April 28, 1971 (with Kissinger)

Nixon: Steve has done a good job.

Listening to the tapes, I was struck by how the ghost of Nixon still affected me. Hearing his very bad, bad, and good moods, even after all those years and history, I found how hurt I was by the first opinion and how relieved by the third!

Another thing I learned many years after the conference: Kitty Kelley, in her 2010 biography *Oprah*, wrote that her subject, then seventeen, was a delegate from Tennessee to the White House Conference on Youth. This was quite a surprise to the national chairman! I still wonder how, if at all, that event in 1971 might have affected this remarkable woman? I wrote to her at her TV program, but she probably never got my letter. If

April 17, 1970

MEMORANDUM FOR :   MR. EHRLICHMAN

The question arises as to whether or not we could move Steve Hess
out of the post he is now in and perhaps back to Harvard. Recognizing
there are great potential problems in this, the question is whether there
are not even potential problems in not doing it.

H. R. HALDEMAN

anyone reading this book knows how to reach Oprah, I would love help in my quest.

What Next?

Of all the top White House aides, Peter Flanigan was probably the least known. A former Wall Street investment banker and longtime Nixon supporter, he had in his portfolio overseeing high-level political appointments. So his call was expected. Would I like to be an ambassador? It can't be Europe, he said. How about a small African country? About 70 percent of ambassadorial posts are distributed to the Foreign Service, the other 30 percent to political supporters and donors. Usually the great capitals, London or Paris, go to the very rich, who can afford the requisite embassy entertaining. (Or as John Adams said to his son John Quincy as he was leaving for London, "Their coachmen and footmen will look down on yours with the utmost scorn and contempt.") Sometimes true experts, who have advised presidential candidates, get appointed. Otherwise it is a collection of people to whom favors are owed. I appreciated Peter's offer, knowing there was no shortage of supplicants. I supposed it would be fun to be called "His Excellency," but I had two small children, an aging mother, and absolutely no professional knowledge of Africa. The decision was not difficult. I thanked Peter and declined the offer.

I kept busy doing a short time study for the White House on the financing of arts institutions in the District of Columbia. Len Garment, Nixon's former law partner and counsel, told me, "It's a big government, lots of jobs." He was only partly right. In the middle of an administration there were not a lot of *good* jobs available. Then Len, a great supporter of the arts, found one—chairman of the National Endowment for the Humanities, created by Congress in 1965 along with its twin, the National Endowment for the Arts, overseeing all federal spending in their respective fields, both in academe and in communities. He informed the Senate Committee on Labor and Public Welfare that I was going to be the president's number one choice.

The right wing was not happy. *Human Events*, the conservative weekly, remembered me from assisting Moynihan in the fight over the "radical" Family Assistance Plan and then being behind the "leftist" resolutions of the White House conferences. Pat Buchanan wrote to Ehrlichman to say that he was "opposed to my friend Steve on ideological grounds." I understood, though was sad he could not tell me to my face.

Those responses were mild compared to what was coming from the organizations gathered under the banner of the American Council of Learned Societies. Its president, Frederick Burkhardt, told the *New York Times* that I was "a disaster" and "totally unqualified." Adding insult to injury, my photograph in the *Times* was captioned "Termed 'Unqualified.'" The harsh language boiled down to—in the words of Yale professor and historian C. Vann Woodward—"[We] have a right to expect that the director should have some clear personal identification with one of the disciplines in the humanities." Or as my friend Arthur Peterson at Ohio Wesleyan reminded me, it was my lack of a "plumber's license."

The next day a story in the *Times* appeared with the headline "Hess 'Saddened' by Opposition to Him for Humanities Post." I was quoted in the article as saying, "It would appear that they are now organizing a campaign to publicly convict me of guilt by nonassociation. . . . I am saddened that some gentlemen who represent the community of scholars would apparently not choose to have read my books so that they might have judged my capacity for scholarship. I am further saddened that they would not have sought an interview so as to ascertain my views on Federal involvement in the humanities." I might have survived the professors' assaults if I had had the backing of the Senate subcommittee leaders, Democrat Claiborne Pell and Republican Jacob Javits. Pell was enthusiastic. Afterward he sent me a letter: "May I congratulate you on the manner in which you conducted yourself during a time when you must have felt the personal nature of the attack. I am truly sorry that it did not work out otherwise." Javits, the most liberal Republican in the Senate, however, issued a form letter of limited interest in the matter. The one time I spoke with him (not in his office, but by chance on a plane), I told him if not me, count on the administration nominating a conservative (which it did in Ronald S. Berman), but he seemed to have no interest in this possibility. John Osborne, who wrote "The Nixon Watch" column in the *New Republic* and who seemed to know more about what was happening in the White House than the rest of us, wrote, "Ehrlichman decided that Mr. Nixon should not be committed to battle in behalf of Hess, despite his acknowledged talents and his past services to the President. Typically of the Nixon procedure in such matters, the choice of whether to stand by Hess or to find a nominee who would be acceptable to the hungry academics was never put up to the President. Ehrlichman made the choice for him." I asked that my name be withdrawn from consideration. It was time to leave.

Leave-Taking, 1972

It had been two packed years. The president invited me to bring my family to the White House to say good-bye. It was late afternoon, January 13, and we were his last appointment before he departed for Ottawa to meet with Canadian prime minister Pierre Trudeau.

We were ushered into the Oval Office. It had been redecorated since I knew it in the Eisenhower years. The flooring with the cleat marks from Ike's golf shoes had been removed and the floor covered with a royal blue rug with the presidential seal. On the wall was the obligatory Gilbert Stuart full-length "Lansdowne" portrait of George Washington (he made three copies). New presidents choose among the presidential desks available, and Nixon was proud of choosing a Wilson desk. (Bill Safire had the unfortunate task of telling Nixon that the desk had belonged to Henry Wilson, vice president under Ulysses S. Grant, not Woodrow Wilson, one of his favorite presidents.) The new decorators from New York had added lots of gold. My eight-year-old son Jamie was rubbing his eyes. We were in one of the world's most famous rooms, but it was not a setting in which a stranger feels comfortable or unimpressed. It was easy to see why Nixon preferred to use it mostly for ceremonial purposes and

"Jamie, I didn't know that you wanted the president's autograph."
"I didn't, Daddy. I wanted the astronaut's!"

moved staff meetings and paperwork to an office across the street in the Executive Office Building.

The president gave us little gifts, things with a presidential seal, tie clips, cuff links, earrings. He repeated jokes he had told many times, and tried small talk—not what he did best.

"What is your favorite subject in school?" the president asked ten-year-old Charlie.

"Geography," Charlie replied.

The president was suddenly animated: "That was my favorite too!"

He now took Charlie on a tour around the perimeter of the Oval Office. He showed off his treasured gifts from other countries. This is a bonsai tree from China!

The military aide looked anxious; our visit was running longer than scheduled. Through a window we could see a helicopter on the South Lawn waiting to take off for Andrews Air Force Base. But it must wait. The Republican chief executive gathered Charles and James Hess around him for his parting words: "You must travel when you are young. Even if you have to borrow the money." He illustrated this by imitating an old man with an imaginary cane trying to maneuver his way down a cruise ship gangplank. This was funny. We were laughing.

That was the last time I would be with Richard Nixon.

Brookings

Robert S. Brookings, born in 1859, left school at sixteen, went to work for a St. Louis company selling woodenware and cordage—household items like clothespins, twine, and brooms—and retired from the company in his late forties with a fortune in excess of $6 million. He arrived in Washington during World War I as a dollar-a-year man to serve on the War Industries Board, concluded that the federal government should do better, dedicated himself to doing something about it, and never left Washington. Ultimately, in 1927 he brought together three organizations whose objectives were understanding economic forces and government organization. His design included a short-lived graduate school that awarded Ph.D.s. Thus was born the Brookings Institution. (Not the Brookings Institute!)

In the vernacular, Brookings is a "think tank," a term with many definitions. The humorist Dave Barry wrote in 1994 that a think tank—and Brookings in particular—was "where people sit around and think during working hours."

I pretend to be embarrassed when Brookings is called, as it was by the *New York Times* in 2016, "the most prestigious think tank in the world." This ignores its history. As James Allen Smith stated in the fine book he wrote for Brookings's seventy-fifth anniversary in 1991, "During the 1930s . . . Brookings made a considerable name for itself, earning a reputation as a locus of opposition to Franklin D. Roosevelt's recovery and reform programs. Later commentators recognized Brookings as a bitter opponent of Harry Truman's efforts to expand the New Deal's social agenda." The prospects for Brookings's survival, wrote its historian, "looked very bleak" until a new president, Robert Calkins, started a rebuilding program in 1952. (He retained only eight of the institution's twenty senior fellows.) In turn, Calkins picked Kermit Gordon as his successor—first as vice president in 1965, then as president in 1967. Kermit had been an economics professor at Williams College when, in 1961, he joined President John F. Kennedy's Council of Economic Advisers, moving to director of the budget the next year. He was retained by President Lyndon B. Johnson, who in 1965 asked him to become secretary of the treasury. Kermit chose Brookings instead.

The Brookings of the 1970s had assets around $50 million. (Multiply by at least ten to estimate Brookings's assets today.) When Richard Nixon was elected president in 1968, Kermit set out to lure his Kennedy-Johnson colleagues to Brookings. He was especially proud of getting Arthur Okun, chairman of the Council of Economic Advisers, who was preparing to return to Yale but could not resist the offer of a six-month "trial marriage" with no strings attached. Okun had a duty, Kermit argued, to write about his experiences as chairman "while the memories were fresh and the wounds unhealed." Art Okun never returned to New Haven.

Kermit's Brookings, which I was about to join, was in the process of moving slightly left of center politically. It was to settle there. Regardless of right-wing cant, as Henry Aaron observed, Brookings's range is somewhere between K and P in the political alphabet.

Settling In

I was thirty-eight in January 1972 when I moved into a sixth-floor office in Brookings's eight-story yellow concrete building at 1775 Massachusetts Avenue, NW. You did not exactly apply to join Brookings—there

_aucet flaw
25. Plan component
26. Type of mortgage: Abbr.
27. Parting word
28. Getting ___ years
29. Like omelets
31. Milk order

40. New St. Louis team
41. Habeas corpus is one
42. Steve at Brookings
44. Scrooge comment
45. Latham of Iowa
46. ___ out a living
47. Tyrannosaurus ___

New contest, winners

Michael Arko is the winner of last week's HillWord contest. His winning entry was drawn at random from a pool of 93 correct solutions faxed to the Hill. Michael works in the library of the Congressional Budget Office, and no matter which numbers you use, he earned a $25 gift certificate to The Trover Shop with which he may do as he pleases.

Answers to last week's puzz

were no forms to fill out or presentations to give. The recruitment system at the time might be described as "circling." You circled the prospective employer, the prospective employer circled you, until both employer and employee agreed that employment was right or wrong. I was offered the choice of senior fellow in the Governmental Studies program (now called Governance Studies) or vice president of the institution. The latter was a complete surprise. I did not seek to come to Brookings to be an administrator, and so my decision was an easy one.

There were then three research programs—Economic Studies, Governmental Studies, and Foreign Policy Studies—but there was no doubt that Brookings's glitter was coming from the economists. Director Joe Pechman was in command of tax policy. Kermit had added Alice Rivlin and Charles Schultze from government. Charlie had succeeded Kermit as President Johnson's budget director. Alice was constantly in and out of government during her many years at Brookings and would become the founding director of the Congressional Budget Office in 1975. Henry Aaron, the social security expert, came from the University of Maryland; George Perry, from the University of Minnesota, joined Okun in creating the esteemed *Brookings Papers on Economic Activity*. Even though I could not understand the numbers they spoke, I enjoyed forty years of lunching with them—and several other economists who came later, such as Barry Bosworth and Gary Burtless—in the Brookings cafeteria. Why eat out?

In case we lacked enough opportunities to listen to each other, Joe Pechman invented the Friday Lunch, a weekly invitation to staff and guests to gather around a massive mahogany table in a darkly paneled room to discuss the issues of the day. I remember Sam Beer, an iconic Harvard professor famous for studying British politics, remarking after one Friday session: "At the Harvard Faculty Club we note a pleasant meal and go back to our offices. Here you get up from the table and declare, 'What are we going to do about it!'"

Governmental Studies

In his reorganization of the Institution, Kermit had chosen Gilbert Y. Steiner to be the director of Governmental Studies. Gil clearly reflected what Kermit was looking for: persons proven in applied research—no theorists need apply—who, if they came out of a university, should also have had experience in some practical aspects of governing. Gil, a professor at the University of Illinois and director of its Institute of Government and Public Affairs, had worked in the Illinois legislature and for the state government; he had also written books on social welfare policy.

Gil, in turn, sought similar qualifications in those he would choose. He was a tough student of how to make the cut, with his own Steiner law: never underestimate another person's insecurity. Gil's program was the smallest: five in Governmental Studies to the fifteen senior people in Economic Studies.

Of the five of us—Steiner, Herbert Kaufman, Martha Derthick, James Sundquist, and me—the most academically established was Herb Kaufman. He had been chairman of the Department of Political Science at Yale before coming to Brookings in 1969. Herb had co-authored a classic study of political power in the modern metropolis, *Governing New York City*. Martha Derthick, who succeeded Gil as director in 1978, went on to the University of Virginia in 1983 to become the Julia Allen Cooper Professor of Government and Foreign Affairs. In 1979 she published by far the greatest policy book any of us have, *Policymaking for Social Security*.

Jim Sundquist, the least academic of us (other than me), seems to have done everything it was possible to do in government before coming to Brookings in 1965: speechwriting for President Truman, secretary to New York governor W. Averell Harriman, administrative assistant to Pennsylvania senator Joseph Clark, deputy under secretary of agriculture in the Johnson administration. Still, he had never written a book on public policy, which was the true business of Brookings. Yet Brookings guessed correctly—and Jim went on to produce six sometimes brilliant studies. Jim followed Martha as the director of Governmental Studies in 1983, before retiring in 1985.

The five of us became six when Richard Nathan arrived in late 1972. Like me, he was another Nixon administration veteran, a key player in the development of the Family Assistance Plan as deputy under secretary at the Department of Health, Education and Welfare. His work at Brookings was different, however: he had grants from the Labor and Commerce Departments to monitor various employment and training programs. He went on to a professorship at Princeton and later became director of the Rockefeller Institute of Government in Albany. Governmental Studies would add another active Republican in 1977, when James Reichley came from President Gerald Ford's White House. Jim's interests included the history of religion in American public life.

What was special about these early years was how much we liked each other. We entertained in our homes and did non-Brookings things together. We were even proud of what our colleagues were producing, which was not something I had often noticed in other parts of the academic world. Governmental Studies was to continue to attract some remarkable directors—notably Tom Mann, who found magical ways to expand the program during financially lean years, and Darrell West, who wisely added the Center for Technology Innovation to our intellectual mandate.

Kermit had promised that Brookings would be "a bridge between the world of ideas and the world of action," and looking back on my first years I could see there was a different texture in my life from the world I had known in high-energy politics. Politics was peaks and valleys. I had not underappreciated the peaks, but what I was now into was a smoothing out. Age was not yet a factor. I liked to think my down-sloping energy line would cross my up-sloping wisdom line at age forty-two. Still time! Rather, I was suddenly luxuriating among interesting people, testing new notions, in a respected organization that did not impose unreasonable restrictions on what I wanted to do.

I started by writing an essay that would grow into a short book, published in 1974 as *The Presidential Campaign: The Leadership Selection Process after Watergate*. It was a modest way to get started, a way of leading up to the book I really wanted to write about the presidency.

I appreciated the Brookings Institution Press, whose publisher, editors, and other worriers were within shouting distance of helping me. We would do seventeen books together and quite a number of revised editions. New versions of *The Presidential Campaign* came out in 1978 and 1988—the latter with a cover by my son Charlie, now a professional graphic designer in Los Angeles.

Perhaps my path from politico to public person was clearest in 1973 when the mayor of Washington, Walter Washington, appointed me to the city's Board of Higher Education. The board was responsible for the oversight of two entities—the District of Columbia Teachers College, which traced its history back to the Normal School for Colored Girls, founded in 1851, and the Federal City College, a four-year liberal arts college opened in 1968. The board's objective was to merge the two institutions with the congressionally administered Washington Technical Institute to form the University of the District of Columbia. The consolidation would eventually be approved in 1975.

I was sworn in at the District Building on Pennsylvania Avenue on March 8, and through the end of the year I attended twenty-four board meetings, thirteen personnel committee meetings, six executive committee meetings, two meetings each of the student affairs, faculty contracts, and education policy committees, and one community relations committee meeting. There was also a graduation at the Teachers College and a Christmas party. As a rule of thumb, any organization that requires fifty meetings in ten months is in trouble. And the trouble is multiplied when there are two schools and two governments, the Congress of the United States being sometimes overly interested in what the District's government was trying to do.

Creating the nation's last land-grant university was a magnificent goal, and I doubt it could have been accomplished—at least in the limited time we had—without Flaxie Pinkett, our chairwoman. Flaxie had taken over her father's real estate and insurance business and was the first black woman to be admitted to the Washington Board of Realtors, which had denied membership to her father. Flaxie knew everyone who was to be known in Washington, joined everything, and was irrepressible. I cannot imagine anyone else at that time telling an angry group of young men who had grievances before the board to "take off their caps." They did, respectfully. I loved working with her and was deeply honored when she asked me to succeed her as chair. I said no. The leader, in this place and at this time, had to be black. The assassination of Martin Luther King Jr. was still too raw in a city whose population, after years of white flight to the suburbs, was over 70 percent black. My five years on the board—I stepped down in 1976—were a profound opportunity for a white man to work and learn and make friends across race lines, which had more roadblocks after Dr. King's death.

Moreover, besides being the nation's capital, Washington was my home. It was where I wanted to live. So with the passage of the District of Columbia Home Rule Act in 1974, which authorized elections for mayor and members of the City Council, I accepted another assignment: to be chairman of a transition commission charged with devising a plan of operations for the incoming City Council. I think our work allowed the new council members, most of whom had never served in a legislature, to get off to a smooth start in January 1975.

One final D.C. item: When, on a brief leave from Brookings in 1976, I was editor in chief of the party platform at the Republican National Convention in Kansas City, the committee endorsed—through a sleight-of-hand that I prefer not to reveal—full congressional voting representation for Washington residents. It was the last time this plank was included in a Republican platform.

Things to Do

Those who work in think tanks learn soon enough that the world is full of billionaires who bequeath their mansions so their former homes can be turned into conference centers for what they consider to be worthy causes. For the attendees, this is usually a very good deal, affording stimulating company and good food, often in an exotic locale. This would be a recurring theme now that I was a worthy. In December 1973, I received an invitation to Arden House, a ninety-six-room mansion fifty miles north of New York City that was built in 1909 for Edward Harriman, the Union Pacific Railroad magnate, and given by his son Averell to Columbia University for public policy discussions under the aegis of Columbia's American Assembly. Our discussion subject: "Choosing the President." We voted against continuing the Electoral College. In 1978 I was part of another panel to discuss the reform of the presidential election process, convened by the Twentieth Century Fund. This time we voted for a modified Electoral College.

Brookings scholars, I quickly realized, are always just back from someplace. Yet this was rarely a topic of conversation at our lunches unless something unfortunate happened. *I got to Suva and it was a national holiday. Everything was closed!* Fiji might have been worth mentioning, but Ames, Iowa? In 1976, I was invited to give a lecture at Iowa State University and insisted it should be on the day before the Iowa caucuses. The students were delighted to be my guide. We went to a high school to watch supporters of competing presidential candidates go through the rituals of telling their neighbors why they preferred Jimmy Carter or Mo Udall or Jerry Brown or someone else, then dividing into groups and reporting their totals, to be passed along to the county convention. I had never felt as proud of being an American.

Watergate

On June 17, 1972, five men were arrested at 2:30 a.m. breaking into the office of the Democratic National Committee at the Watergate hotel and office complex in Washington, an event that pyramided into the most serious political scandal in American history and, just over two years later, produced the only resignation of a U.S. president. Since I had left the White House for Brookings only half a year before and had a connection with many of the main players in this drama, there was no way that Watergate was going to be far from my attention—or me far from a radio or TV interview.

Until Nixon's secret recordings of his White House conversations revealed the answer to what PBS's Robert MacNeil called "the ultimate question"—"How high did the scandals reach, and was President Nixon himself involved?"—there were many possibilities, partly because breaking and entering and similar crimes are not the sorts of things that presidents are known to involve themselves in. They are too smart or too crafty or too otherwise engaged.

I knew which side I wanted to be on. Richard Nixon was a friend—and if it was sometimes a rocky friendship, this was probably more typical of Nixon's friendships than not. I even gave a talk at the Harvard Business School in March 1974 on all the ways and reasons that the awfulness of the crimes that were collectively referred to as "Watergate" could have happened without Nixon's knowledge: Wasn't he consumed by matters of foreign policy? Isn't there a Gresham's law of presidential staffing in which bad staff drives out good? The party would have properly assessed risk, but he removed the campaign from the party. And so forth.

Right down the list, I was dead wrong.

The pain of having to examine what had happened was produced by the Senate Watergate Committee. Nationally televised hearings began on May 18, 1973. Public television put together the team of MacNeil and Jim Lehrer for the first time and offered gavel-to-gavel coverage from the WETA studio just across the Potomac in Arlington, Virginia. After the first week of testimony, the three commercial networks returned to normal programming and rotated daily coverage, thereby cutting their advertising losses by two-thirds. PBS moved ahead on its own, even rebroadcasting the day's hearings in prime time. This meant that its audience was massive: 85 percent of Americans watched some part of the hearings.

MacNeil and Lehrer had two side men, one to offer legal commentary and the other to offer political commentary. The lawyers rotated. I did the politics. The drill went something like this. On July 19, after intense listening, Lehrer turned to me and said, "Clear it all up for us." To which I responded:

Well, having listened in quite short order to Mr. Mitchell and Mr. LaRue and Mr. Mardian, it appears that no one quite remembers the same thing as anyone else remembered it. . . . An interpretation might be found in a political cartoon by the famous Thomas Nast which appeared about a hundred years ago when he was exposing the Tweed Ring in New York City. All of the culprits were standing in a circle, each one was pointing at the other, and the caption read, "He did it." Well, the question of presidential involvements still is going to have to wait until the release of the tapes, but I do think the committee continues to build a very strong case on the obstruction of justice grounds regarding the Watergate cover-up.

By July 23 I was burned out, and I told the anchors I planned to leave the show. For my last appearance, this is how Lehrer introduced me: "Special significance tonight because he is the author of five books and now he's going to finish number six and go back to earning his bread at the Brookings Institution. In short, this is his last day and last night with us on these shows. So, Mr. Hess, what are your thoughts not only at the end of today, but at the end of your session with us?"

This was my verdict:

What really was happening was off camera, the momentous decisions that were being made. And this was the first time in history that the Congress had served a subpoena on the president of the United States. This is a very sad day. It is a very disturbing day. There was nothing exhilarating about this moment. Two great institutions had chosen not to blink. It struck me they had simply run out of good will. There was no willingness left to accommodate, particularly on the president's part. There seemed to be an impurity of motives, a loss and lack of trust and respect. I think this can only be remembered in history as a very nasty day for America. So I'm glad to be leaving. . . . I've enjoyed my association with you gentlemen, but I must admit I haven't liked wallowing in this filth. I feel unclean even listening. I don't think that many of these witnesses really understand what this country is all about—differences and diversities and respect for each other that makes the country operate. I don't even like listening to myself talking about it. I sound like a narrow prig. I'm mad at these people, and I sound mean, and I don't think of myself as a mean person. So tonight as I leave you I'm distressed, and I'm burned out, and I salute you for performing a very useful though distressing service, and I wish you fortitude and a strong stomach.

Nixon had taped his conversations to provide the material for his memoir, I believe, not for nefarious reasons. Yet these tapes revealed the actions that ultimately destroyed him, his presidency, and the men around him. I often wonder about "the men around him," products of solid middle- or upper-middle-class families who went to elite schools like Brown, Williams, and the University of Southern California, yet were trapped in "Nixon's web" and went to prison for their loyalty. Still, not every loyalist chose to be involved. Pat Buchanan rejected the assignment that sent Egil "Bud" Krogh to prison.

They did not all have the same motivations. Bob Haldeman, Nixon's chief of staff, was the long and true believer. His wife, Jo, in a moving book, wrote of her state of mind in 1971: "Bob's commitment to a cause larger than himself is so strong and all-consuming, I sometimes think that I might be losing him to President Nixon." White House Counsel Chuck Colson was very different from Haldeman. He was ruthless and set out to gain status with Nixon by performing "dirty tricks" that could advance him over his competitors. Even in his best-selling memoir *Born Again,* he recounted how he had tried to destroy Arthur Burns, Nixon's domestic adviser, in 1971. Jeb Magruder was a simpler story. Several years after Watergate, I was having lunch at the Federal City Club when Jeb entered, spotted me, and made a beeline for my table. "The next time you write about me, instead of sayings I'm foolish and immoral just say I'm dumb." I stood corrected. Saddest to me is Krogh, another young man who believed he had to do his assignment if the president considered it critical to national security. Krogh's "plumbers"—they fixed leaks—broke into the office of the psychiatrist of Daniel Ellsberg in search of material to discredit the man who leaked the Pentagon Papers. When Bud got out of prison, he went to see Nixon in San Clemente. In Bud's sad little book, *Integrity*, he reported that he told Nixon he was proud to have served in the administration and to have taken full responsibility for his actions. Nixon replied that he didn't feel guilty of any crime.

In 1982 Nixon sent me one of his books, in which he had inscribed "To Steve Hess from RN." That evening, at Washington's Arena Theatre, my wife and I saw Bill and Helene Safire during the intermission. "I got a book from RN today," I told them. "What do you think it means?"

"It means he's forgiven you," Helene replied.

Pat Moynihan told me that I needed to have closure with Nixon and that he would arrange for us to go to New Jersey and have lunch. But before we could get there Nixon's memoir, *RN*, was published, offering no apology for his role in the crimes of Watergate—except that he was sorry he had let down the American people. This was good enough for David Frost but not for me.

Talk

For the journalist covering Watergate, which was virtually the entire Washington press corps, who better to interview than a person who had recently worked in the Nixon White House *and* now worked for a think tank? Brookings president Kermit Gordon, the man who hired me, could not have been happy. He was too polite to say. But clearly, he did not expect his scholars to hang around broadcast green rooms. Brookings at the time had a communications staff of one, and I do not think our communicator was overworked.

Throughout 1973 the story kept unraveling—H. R. Haldeman and John Ehrlichman resign, John Dean is fired, Alexander Butterfield reveals the existence of a taping system in the president's offices. Nixon refuses to turn over the tapes to the Senate Watergate committee or to

Special Prosecutor Archibald Cox. Nixon fires Cox, prompting Attorney General Elliot Richardson to resign. There is an eighteen-and-a-half-minute gap in the tape during a conversation between Nixon and Haldeman.

And on into 1974—the Supreme Court rules Nixon must turn over the tapes. The House Judiciary Committee passes an article of impeachment. Finally, on August 8, Richard Nixon resigns, and on August 9 Gerald Ford becomes president. A month later, Ford pardons Nixon.

As Watergate moved from current events to history, talk became a measurable part of my job description. A third of my workday was spent responding to calls from reporters—less in odd-numbered years, more in even-numbered, election years. I had become, in the words of a Washington magazine, "a world-class sound-biter." The celebrity part of this occupation was nice, up to a point, though I was uncomfortable being recognized by strangers in public places (a sensible test for anyone in a position to adjust their prominence).

Yet I liked talking and was good at it. On one occasion the phone rang at a quarter past one in the morning of January 19, 1990. It was a Reuters reporter telling me that the mayor of Washington, Marion Barry, had been arrested in the Vista Hotel on a drug charge. According to my wife, I said, "If what you tell me is true, this is a sad day for Marion Barry and the people of the District of Columbia." The next morning I had no recollection of the phone ringing. I had given a sound bite in my sleep.

I never mistook this for an exalted goal, but I always tried to help reporters put their stories in a proper context, especially those from other countries. Most questioners needed nothing deeper than a snap reaction to a morning headline. Still, there were times when a question was intriguing, as when a *Philadelphia Inquirer* reporter wanted to know the reasons for the disappearance of presidents' beards. My answer: "For some, beards equal intellectuals and we certainly don't want intellectuals in the White House. They scare us. Another image might be hippie or counterculture, and we certainly don't want them."

At the end of 1996, a presidential election year, my assistant, Pat Fowlkes, compiled a list of 276 news organizations that had interviewed me at least once in the preceding twelve months. Between October 21 and November 8, I had to stay home after a cancer operation, and Pat turned the basement into a makeshift studio from which I did 119 interviews—thirteen television (including Norway, Germany, the Netherlands, Korea, and Japan), nineteen radio (including Britain, Australia, and the Netherlands), and the rest print (including interviews with reporters from Austria, Finland, Colombia, and France). Brookings's president Michael Armacost sent me a note: "Steve, some recuperation!"

What might Google make of all this? I type "Stephen Hess quotes" into the search function and get back a steady stream of words I have said, all shorn of context—dates, sources, and such.

Hess quote: "If she had just gone home I think she would have been remembered importantly, but she didn't just go home." (Who is she? Where is home? Why didn't she go?)

Worthless for research, but might suggest a Quotes game. Each player gets one minute to explain the quote:

Hess quote: "Besides, he's already spoken extensively about the hurricanes."

Player 1: Look, Will, try again. You've already used hurricanes in one play.

Player 2: Maybe Columbus does need more money, Isabella, but he's already used the hurricanes gambit.

Player 3: Listen, Coach, Hurricanes is a bad name for your team even if it is in South Florida.

All this talking ultimately dominated the opinion news programs that fueled cable television. Was this why I came to Brookings? I appeared once on CNN's *Crossfire*. The subject was bland enough, "The Two-Party System." And my opponent was a friend, John Anderson, who had run as an independent for president in 1980. After the two picadors, Bob Novak and Michael Kinsley, did their job and sufficiently enraged us, John and I started shouting at each other. The producers loved it. I was mortified. If I leave only one quote to history, please remember: "It doesn't make any difference what you wear on radio or what you say on television." You can quote me.

The Presidency Book

My book *Organizing the Presidency* was published just before the 1976 election—and it produced for me all that I wanted in coming to Brookings. The book was praised by some people I greatly admired (John Osborne in the *New Republic* called it "magnificent"); it was attacked by some people I greatly admired (Rexford Tugwell, also in the *New Republic,* wrote that my "prescription has already been tried and rejected"). And it was praised and attacked by people who had not read it, which is still a good sign that a book is making an impact. I cherished most a long unsolicited letter from Peter Drucker, who was by then America's foremost author on management theory: "I am quite convinced that you are right. And I am quite convinced that you are futile. You are trying to square the circle—that is to make the President capable of being the maker of policy and of vision, and yet maintain the full activities of today's government. This, my dear Mr. Hess, cannot and will not work." The book became a main selection of the Fortune Book Club and an alternate selection of the Book-of-the-Month Club.

Organizing the Presidency describes the White House through the terms of six presidents, Roosevelt to Nixon. Having served in two presidential administrations—one at the end, one at the beginning—I could not escape seeing that beginnings and endings are different. This led to an opening chapter drawing a "composite president"—what the presidency looks like to a president in year one, year two, year three, and so on. As such, I was writing outside the more traditional framework at the time of the powers of the presidency or the history of a single president or single topic.

Soon after the book was published, my own story took another sudden twist. Late in the summer of 1976, President Ford appointed me to serve on the U.S. delegation to the UN General Assembly. On Friday, November 19, I was in my office at the U.S. delegation headquarters in New York City. My secretary came into the office to tell me that Governor Carter was calling. I don't know a Governor Carter. Then it dawned on me: "You mean *that* Governor Carter?" She nodded her head: yes.

This was a time when Jimmy Carter carried his own suitcase and personally called folks who were not expecting to get a call from the president-elect. He had read my book and wanted help immediately. The next day I flew to Washington and met with Dick Cheney, the outgoing president's chief of staff, who spent two and a half hours with me going over White House operations office by office. I then reported to the incoming president on how he could make seventy-seven staff reductions when he took office. The second edition of *Organizing the Presidency*, published in 1988, was expanded to include an appendix of the twelve memos I wrote for Carter and another appendix on transition planning for President-elect Reagan in 1980. The third edition, published in 2002 in collaboration with the presidential scholar James P. Pfiffner of George Mason University, extended the book to the beginning of President George W. Bush's first term.

Pat Moynihan, who had just been elected to the U.S. Senate in November 1976, surprised me by sending Carter a letter urging him to hire me. Carter replied, "I really appreciate your writing me about Steve Hess. He has been helping me a great deal the past few weeks, and I share your deep respect for his abilities. You can be assured that I will give him every consideration for a position in my administration." This gave me the excuse to politely tell Carter that I was not interested in leaving Brookings. I did, however, agree to a part-time consultancy for a couple of months to work on his reorganization plan. As James Fallows put it in the May 1979 issue of *The Atlantic*, this was because Carter had "eagerly [accepted] a naïve book by Stephen Hess."

Newswork

What should I do next?

While I enjoyed attention as the author of a prominent book, I recognized the powerful draw of the presidency—almost a cultlike attraction that seemed to have sucked some serious writers into a revolving world of conferences and media appearances at the expense of productive research. In the back of my mind: Move away from the presidency, at least for now.

How the press fitted into the web of governance was becoming a subject of special interest to me. The media—as it now likes to be called— had been massively important in the Watergate story and had turned me into a sound bite overnight. I now knew a lot of reporters, but I also knew I had very little knowledge of their world.

If this was going to be my next subject, I had to narrow the focus to the Washington press corps. First, the "literature," the body of work I had to read before getting started. My first surprise was that it did not exist. There was only one book—*The Washington Correspondents,* written in the mid-1930s by Leo Rosten when he was a graduate student at the University of Chicago—and one article, a reconsideration of Rosten's questions by William Rivers in the *Columbia Journalism Review* in 1962. There were also various reporters' presidents-who-have-known-me books.

So in 1977 I started from scratch—first by interviewing 150 key Washington journalists, then writing a 150-page summary of my observations on how they operated, which I sent to the interviewees for their corrective comments. Now I could really begin. I compiled a list of 1,250 reporters who covered the national government for commercial news outlets in the United States. I discovered that journalists are ill at ease with abstractions, so I devised a "daily log" that asked them for precise information on each story they filed. What events attended? Documents used? Types of people (not by name) interviewed? On or off the record? Over half the reporters agreed to be part of my enterprise. I also conducted a telephone survey, assisted by six interns, asking open-ended questions, such as what, if any, are the political biases of the press corps? The third piece of the project was coding a week's worth of stories—2,022 in all—that appeared in twenty-two newspapers and a weekly newsmagazine and on three television networks. The objective was to sort out this massive collection of words by institutions and subjects. The reporters' logs represented what went into a story; the story analysis was what came out. If I made one mistake in this project, it was offering the reporters anonymity, thinking it would improve my response rate. I never made this mistake again—they loved my quoting them by name. *The Washington Reporters,* published in 1981, became the first of seven books that collectively I named *Newswork.*

Two subsequent titles related to Congress—*The Ultimate Insiders: U.S. Senators in the National Media,* published in 1986, and *Live from Capitol Hill! Studies of Congress and the Media,* which appeared in 1991. The Senate Press Gallery privately kept a record of every TV camera at Senate hearings (probably to justify its budget). With permission, I sent my interns to Capitol Hill to sort them out by subject to illustrate the media's priorities. The fun is always in finding new data and new ways to use them. I examined the minutes of the self-governing congressional press galleries to see how the watchdogs watched themselves. I compared the salaries of press secretaries to those of other staffers and then compared their place in the office hierarchy to what they told me their place was. I snared senators coming from meetings and introduced myself (which was more efficient than making appointments). "The press will put an adjective in front of your name, Senator. If you had your druthers, what adjective would you choose?" They loved this question and often stopped to give me a long answer. Their favorite adjective was "hardworking"—most revealing! After a senator invited me to a screening room to watch him enjoying himself on television, I titled one chapter, "I Am on TV, Therefore I Am." I added up how often House members appeared on the television news in their district: not often, though they preferred to believe otherwise.

In *The Government/Press Connection: Press Officers and Their Offices,* which Brookings published in 1984, I spent a year inside five government agencies—the White House, State Department, Department of Defense, Department of Transportation, and the Food and Drug Administration. Site observation was a different type of research, and after I received my security clearance I was amazed at my access. To the best of my knowledge, the only meetings I was excluded from were those of supervisors evaluating the merits of their employees. For my chapter "Leaks and Other Informal Communications," I devised a typology of leaks by cause: the Ego Leak, the Goodwill Leak, the Policy Leak, the Animus Leak, the Trial-Balloon Leak, and the Whistle-Blower Leak. (The Ego Leak is the most common, designed to massage the leaker's sense of importance with a gift of information.) There was also the unexpected, as when I witnessed a tragedy in which seventy-eight people died in a plane crash. On January 13, 1982, I was with the secretary of transportation when—literally outside his window—an Air Florida jet crashed just after takeoff into the 14th Street Bridge over the icy Potomac. I watched hour by hour at the government's center as men and women responded to the crisis. The case study I wrote was about how quickly and competently they responded with lives on the line.

In 1996's *International News & Foreign Correspondents*, I asked what events beyond the United States were covered in the American media, and what did we know about the men and women doing the reporting. Were they married? If so, to another journalist? Did they have children? Not irrelevant questions. Family considerations can affect assignments. Steven Weisman and Elisabeth Bumiller—he with the *New York Times*, she then with the *Washington Post*—chose to wait until they left India and were reassigned to Japan before having a child. Tokyo, Beijing, Vienna, Prague, Jerusalem, Istanbul were among the points on my itinerary. John Pomfret, in Bosnia for the *Washington Post*, advised, "Never wash your car. If someone plants a bomb under it, you'll see fingerprints." In Tel Aviv, Bob Simon of CBS News was impatient for something newsworthy to happen. "Bob, it's only been four months since the last crisis," I said. He shrugged, "Hey, we're talking news." Dealing with danger in Lebanon, E. J. Dionne, Jr.—then in Rome with the *New York Times*—recalled, "You get hooked on your own adrenalin." Nick

Kristof, as a correspondent for the *Times* in Beijing, recalled his expense account after the 1989 Tiananmen Square protests: "One bike run over by tank." Sylvia Poggioli, covering the Balkan war for National Public Radio, described a dangerous moment when she was traveling with photographers, for whom getting close to the action is an occupational hazard. I interviewed a lot of fatalists—and a lot of brave people.

In *Through Their Eyes: Foreign Correspondents in the United States*, published in 2005, I charted how these journalists, bunched in New York and Washington, need events like a presidential election to feel the rest of the country. My "Hollywood" chapter recounted the odd history of the Hollywood Foreign Press Association, whose members vote for the Golden Globes. There were eighty-two active members when I did my interviewing in 1999, a majority of whom write pop-culture pieces like "Nicole Kidman Is the Epitome of Class" (for Singapore's *Solitaire* magazine) or "How Could I Not Accept an Invitation from Warner Brothers Studio to Visit the Sets of the [Harry Potter] Film in London" (for India's *Mid-Day* newspaper).

For the 2000 presidential election I decided to study television network news coverage in real time. My assistant, Jessica Gerrity, with a team of three, taped all campaign stories broadcast on ABC, CBS, NBC, and PBS news shows between Labor Day and Election Day. This was to be the distillate of what Americans were to learn from TV news about candidates George W. Bush and Al Gore. It also formed the basis of my weekly column, "The Hess Report," which appeared every Monday in *USA Today*. My comments were highly critical—two-thirds of the news stories were devoted to the candidates' strategies and only one-third to substance. But I also wanted to find a way to acknowledge some excellent journalism, so I self-invented prizes for four types of stories. My Governance Award was given to the story I judged most helpful in informing voters of how a candidate might perform as president; the Campaign Award related more specifically to the events of the week; the Interview Award recognized the skill of the interviewer; and the Fred Friendly Award, named for the former president of CBS News, recognized long-form journalism. Among the winners were Martha Raddatz of ABC News for a story on military readiness, NBC's Claire Shipman on the entertainment industry's connection with Al and Tipper Gore in "A Cozy and Profitable Relationship with Hollywood," and Leslie Stahl's segment for *60 Minutes* called "Testing, Testing, Testing," laying out the pros and cons of Bush's proposed education reforms. I never imagined that my personal opinions would turn into a network competition until ABC started advertising that it had won Hess Awards!

Not long after finishing *Through Their Eyes*, I was given an opportunity to write about my research while ensconced in a sixteenth-century Lombard villa atop a hill in Bellagio, looking down on Lake Como, at the northern tip of Italy. Villa Serbelloni—it is beautiful! The home of Her Serene Highness, Ella, Principessa della Torre e Tasso, born Ella Walker, heiress to the Hiram Walker fortune, who gave her estate to the Rockefeller Foundation, in 1960 it became the Bellagio Study and Conference Center. The guests are given a month in residence (mine was May 2007), with a bedroom, an office, excellent meals, and instructions that this is not a vacation, you must work all day. One difference from my other conference center experiences was that we were not all media or presidency people. We included a poet, an artist designing a painting out of bird feathers, a musician composing an opera, and scholars of Blake, neurotropic viral infections, and tap dancing. Besides Americans (a majority), we came from Bulgaria, India, Russia, and Israel. We had so much to say to each other—but no shop talk. It was wonderful.

Finally, I published *Whatever Happened to the Washington Reporters 1978–2012*, the last of the *Newswork* series, in which I set out to find the 450 Washington reporters I first surveyed in 1978. With my intrepid team of interns—Nathaniel Lubin (Harvard), Elizabeth Krevsky (Cornell), Lynda Marlow (BBC), and Sarah Lovenheim (George Washington University)—and my teaching assistant, Michelle Begnoche, we tracked them down in France, England, Italy, Australia, and nineteen U.S. states, with many still in the Washington area. We located 90 percent of them and interviewed 283, producing the first comprehensive study of career patterns in American journalism. Journalists, as expected, proved to be great storytellers. Judy Woodruff, the anchor of the PBS *NewsHour*, recalled her early days: "It was like a Cinderella story. During the week I would come in and be the secretary in the newsroom, and then on Sunday night I would come in at six, and for five hours I would pore over the weather wires, and then I learned how to do the weather reports." Bernard Kalb, once a reporter for CBS, NBC, and the *New York Times*, recounted his resignation as State Department spokesman after learning that the Reagan administration had conducted a disinformation campaign to mislead the press about Libyan leader Muammar Gaddafi. On November 24, 1963, CBS's Ike Pappas told of being live on the radio as Jack Ruby brushed past him to shoot Lee Harvey Oswald: "Could this possibly be the assassin of the United States president now being killed? Put that in words. And I just said what I saw." The transcripts of the interviews are in the Manuscript Division in the Library of Congress (available without my permission).

In the foreword to the first volume of the *Newswork* books, Bruce MacLaury, president of the Brookings Institution in 1981, wrote, "In the vast literature about how Americans govern themselves, the role of the press is often neglected. Yet the press—no less than the presidency, the judiciary, and the legislature—is a public policy institution and deserves a place in the explanations of governmental process." Twenty-four years later, in the foreword to the sixth *Newswork* volume, Strobe Talbott, president of Brookings in 2005, reflected on MacLaury's words: "It's hard to imagine that statement being made today, given the cottage industry press watching has become, including in think tanks like this one. Yet Bruce was accurately reflecting the degree to which the media was then at the margins of social science scholarship."

I am fortunate to have been in the thick of this scholarly uprising, advising along the way what became the Shorenstein Center on Media, Politics and Public Policy at Harvard, where my close friend Marvin Kalb became its first director in 1986, followed by Alex Jones in 2000. The initial spark for press studies came from Jonathan Moore, who became director of the Kennedy School's Institute of Politics in 1974. Asked by Moore, I commuted to Cambridge for three years to teach a course on the media. Previously Harvard had been without a media offering.

Media studies could not have been so comfortably settled into Harvard's world without the skill and caring of Marvin, Alex, and Jonathan.

In 1981, I wrote, "Journalists are great fun to study." I am proud to have been right.

Transitions

In the forty-eight years between John F. Kennedy's election and the election of Barack Obama, there have been eight periods known as presidential transitions—the time between the election and the inauguration of a new president. I was involved, in one way or another, in all eight.

The nearly three-month period from early November until January 20 is a rare gift of startup time that I do not think is offered to a leader in any other country. The White House is symbolically emptied as the old president moves out and the new president, with new people, moves in. Who are they? What might they tell us about the future? Do they fit together or not? Priorities . . . pace . . . surprises. Count the ways. The attention of Main Street and the media may never be as keen. Do we exaggerate signs of initial success or troubling error?

Running the executive branch of the U.S. government is a vast job and a great honor. Surely the aspirants will have given considerable thought to what they will do once they are in office. The record suggests otherwise. What they do is give considerable thought to how to get elected. They may leave a few aides at home to compile lists of names for postelection planning, but little else.

Our recent presidents carried impressive credentials: governors, senators; two had even served as vice president for eight years. Yet each made transition mistakes that would plague them in office: a disastrous incursion of Cuba, Senate confirmation defeat of a candidate for defense secretary, "Nannygate" problems that derailed two nominees for attorney general, a treasury secretary who said he opposed the president's policies, appointments the president soon longs to take back—Les Aspin, Alexander Haig, James Edwards, Walter Hickel.

As part of the departing Eisenhower staff in 1960–61—my first transition—I could feel that the incoming Kennedy people did not much want our help. Too bad. There were lots of White House things that even a lowly speechwriter would have been glad to explain. I was asked only one question. Pierre Salinger, Kennedy's press secretary, wanted to know whether Jim Hagerty, Eisenhower's press secretary, really kept the wire service teletype in his lavatory. Yes, I answered. I could have given him reasons for why this was not a good idea. But he didn't ask. Was this snobbery? The Kennedy people considered the Eisenhower people intellectually irrelevant (there were to be fifteen Rhodes Scholars in Kennedy's administration). Or was this what William Manchester called "generational chauvinism"? Kennedy's people were young, Eisenhower's were not. Still, it is unusual to reject advice, since it costs nothing to listen.

My second transition—Lyndon Johnson to Richard Nixon, in 1968–69—was literally the reverse of eight years earlier, when Eisenhower was leaving and Kennedy arriving. For one thing, I was coming back. Coming back is more fun than leaving. Still, it was a unique round trip. I was joining a Republican White House as an assistant to a Democrat, Daniel Patrick Moynihan. Pat's assignment during the transition was to design and staff a new White House unit, the Urban Affairs Council. In contrast to the experience gap between the Kennedy and Eisenhower people in 1960, Pat knew the federal government from having been an assistant secretary of labor in the Johnson administration and had friendships with experts in the civil service who knew what worked and what didn't. As a result, Nixon's domestic program got off to a fast start, and he was able to sign an executive order creating the Urban Affairs Council as his first act. Regrettably, the signing pen that we gave the president leaked all over his hands.

Earlier in this chapter I told about my third transition, the 1976–77 transition from Gerald Ford to Jimmy Carter, when the president-elect asked my advice on reorganizing the White House. For two months I gladly took calls—even when they were in the middle of Redskins games—and tried to answer his questions. "Should the Office of the

Special Representative for Trade Negotiations be taken out of the Executive Office of the President and put in the Treasury Department?" (No, it works well where it is; moving it would produce a prolonged fight.) The fact that I had been editor in chief of the Republican Party's platform in 1976 did not seem to bother the Carter people. President Ford may have lost the election, but his chief of staff, Dick Cheney, generously provided whatever information Carter requested. This would create the pattern for future transitions—experienced political veterans crossing party lines to help make government work.

Early in 1980, before it was clear who would be the GOP's nominee, Republican National Committee chairman Bill Brock asked me to prepare a paper outlining the necessary elements for putting together a transition, which would be presented to the party's nominee. Ronald Reagan eventually secured the nomination, and he assigned Edwin Meese to direct his pre-election planning. The Meese-planned transition was the best of them all. I do not know if my suggestions helped. Much of my report had focused on things Meese could do before the election, such as preparing a chronological list of the expiration dates of all term appointments, particularly at the regulatory agencies. But there were also lots of questions for Reagan as well, such as on the appointing process: Do you want to give your cabinet officers the authority to choose their own deputy/under/assistant secretaries? Are there any jobs that can be best filled by setting up search committees? When you do not have specific people in mind, what are the most useful questions to ask of candidates for each top job? What positions do you wish to abolish? What precedents need be considered, such as a Western governor for secretary of the interior? There were also several smaller decisions: What pictures do you want to hang on the walls of the Cabinet Room? Which past president's desk do you want in the Oval Office?

For the next three transitions, I was part of constituencies that sought roles in the incoming administration and produced reports for the new president: the public administration professionals; the people who become political executives; and the community of scholars. Each of these constituencies approached the transitions from slightly different angles.

In 1988, the year George H. W. Bush was elected president after serving eight years as Reagan's vice president, the National Academy of Public Administration issued a substantial report on the presidential transition. NAPA is a peer-elected society of which I am a member. One of the committees was chaired by Elmer Staats, who had been comptroller general during four presidential administrations. The Staats Report went beyond the more standard transition subjects of White House organization and political appointments to make recommendations on invigorating the public service, revitalizing federal management, coping with the budget deficit, and gaining congressional cooperation. Bush, as an old hand in the executive branch, was more likely to be attuned to such proposals than either Clinton, the Arkansas governor, or Obama, the first-term senator.

In 1992–93, following Bill Clinton's defeat of President Bush, a "Memorandum for the President-Elect" was prepared by the Carnegie Endowment for International Peace and the Institute for International Economics. This committee was chaired by Richard Holbrooke, a fixture among political executives from the presidencies of Carter to Obama. He was an investment banker when he wasn't in government—and was always talked about as a potential nominee for secretary of state.

Holbrooke's report, unlike Staats's report, was designed for immediate notice by Bill Clinton's inner circle. There were only two Republicans on the commission, myself and the venerable former Minnesota congressman Bill Frenzel, and we enjoyed listening to our colleagues' interventions, which looked a lot like auditioning for a job. Indeed, I now count seven who did get jobs, including Holbrooke, as ambassador to Germany, and Madeleine Albright, as ambassador to the United Nations and later as secretary of state. The commission's principal recommendation, a three-council configuration in the White House—National Security, Economic, Domestic—was in fact adopted by Clinton. This was considered a victory over the reputation of transition reports as dust-gatherers. What I loved about this report was how much it was about titles: "We suggest adding the word 'The' to the titles of these three Presidential aides, and no others, in order to elevate them slightly vis-à-vis other Presidential assistants. . . . Furthermore, previous titles for economic and domestic Presidential aides included qualifying adjectives such as 'policy' or 'strategy.' We suggest these be dropped." There was a whole section called "Title Creep." Since I had once been "Deputy Assistant to the President for Urban Affairs," without an elevating "The," I thoroughly understood the Holbrooke committee's concern.

The studies for the Clinton-to-George W. Bush transition in 2000–01 were prepared by the Brookings Institution under the direction of Governmental Studies chairman Paul C. Light, possibly academia's most careful student of trends in the federal workforce. For this report, my contribution was a long chapter on lessons learned from past transitions, starting with Nixon, in a volume edited by G. Calvin Mackenzie, *Innocent until Nominated: The Breakdown of the Presidential Appointments Process.* I urged presidents-elect to quickly make appointments: the longer the delay, the more pressure they will be under. I urged incoming presidents to make their White House appointments first (Clinton made most of his just days before the inauguration), since they are the processors who must be in place to facilitate the rest of the agenda. I urged making appointments in clusters. How could Carter have imagined a harmonious national security cluster with the hawkish Zbigniew Brzezinski in the White House and the dovish Cyrus Vance at State, according to those who had worked with them? I urged presidents-elect to choose their demographic goals and then add units to the cabinet if necessary. I warned that idle reporters are dangerous reporters during the transition period—and that the press secretary must be prepared to "feed the beast." Finally, I warned that every incoming administration will have one horrendous confirmation fight. Senators seem to demand it. This is not easy for nominees who think they are important. My advice was simple: smile and grovel.

In 2008–09 I offered Barack Obama a transition package of graphs, charts, diagrams, floor plans, case studies, and miscellaneous bits of wisdom and advice in a little book called *What Do We Do Now? A Workbook for the President-Elect.* The title came from the 1972 movie *The Candidate,* when a political neophyte played by Robert Redford, having just won a surprise victory for the U.S. Senate, asks this question of his campaign manager. Among the items in the book:

- A list of questions to ask candidates for White House chief of staff, such as "Can you take the blame for 'forgetting' to invite a major contributor to the state dinner for the Queen of England?"
- A White House office organizational chart with POTUS at the top, continuing down to empty boxes that can be filled in at the bottom.

- Floor plans of the first and second floors of the West Wing, highlighting offices close to the Oval Office.

- A diagram of who sits around the cabinet table during meetings and who sits up against the walls.

- A checklist of what should be completed by Thanksgiving (key national security and economic appointments) and what by Christmas (schedule meetings with budget director to review next year fiscal options, with speechwriters to discuss themes for the inaugural address, and with the White House usher for living arrangements and special needs).

- Photographs of portraits that other presidents have hung in the Oval Office, including three of George Washington. Also, a list of presidential desks.

- Advice for the inauguration, including details about picking a Bible (Franklin Roosevelt took the oath of office on his family's Dutch-language Bible), a biblical passage (optional), the preferred music (Nixon picked "This Is My Country," Carter picked "The

Battle Hymn of the Republic," and Clinton selected "Fanfare for the Common Man"), and the poet (optional).

I had fun with this book—and was proud that a reviewer called it "uncommonly unpretentious."

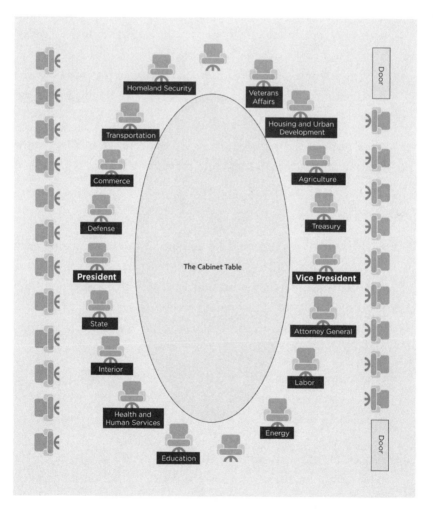

Someone has to tell the president who sits where.
A graphic from What Do We Do Now?

Beth's List: A Summing Up

In 1993 the Cunard Line offered me a ten-day Alaska cruise—whale watching, a helicopter flight over the glaciers and ice fields, a train ride into the Klondike—for which all I had to do was give two lectures. A glorious deal, by my standards. My first lecture was to be on the presidency, the second on the news media. After my presidency performance, I awaited Beth's praise. "Why didn't you tell the story about—? Or the one where—?" Wives of long standing know them all. Apparently, I had failed. So I said, "Make a list." When the audience arrived for the second day, I announced a change of plans. Instead of the "The News Media," the lecture I gave was "Beth's List"—the stories I had left out. (Beth claims that half the audience walked out. Not true!)

Now, after 50,000 words, mostly chronological, Beth is right again. It is time to tell some of the stories I have left out. They won't be in chronological order, and one story doesn't necessarily relate to another— except that it happened to me. Can I tell you about the time I briefly met Admiral Rickover, or danced with Jacqueline Kennedy? Or where I was on September 11, 2001? Or about a desperately ill boy who wanted to be president for a day? Or an idea for Ruth Bader Ginsburg? Reminiscence is good. Our lives are filled with events and people we want to remember.

September 11, 2001

We all live in the backwash of great historical events. For me, the first one was the Japanese bombing of Pearl Harbor, on December 7, 1941, the date that President Roosevelt declared "will live in infamy." It was midafternoon Sunday in New York City, where we lived. I was seven years old. I was playing with a friend in my room, and my parents were in the living room with the parents of my friend. I do not know how they got the news of the attack, but I could see that they were upset. I cannot go beyond the knowledge that I did not know what was happening; still, I vividly live with the impressions of that day.

My impressions of September 11, 2001, shared throughout the world, come from the televised images of planes crashing into New York's World Trade Center buildings. Was it an accident? Within a few minutes we knew it was not. I was supposed to be briefing a group of British parliamentarians at Brookings that Tuesday. But Brookings had just closed. I got through to the State Department escort officer. She was frantic. The group had been expelled from the Senate. I invited them to our apartment for a hastily put-together lunch. We lived on the fourteenth floor. We looked across the Potomac and saw smoke rising from the Pentagon. When the parliamentarians arrived—seven members of the House of Commons and a baroness, along with two State Department officers—we rushed to the windows. What would change? What would remain the same?

A few days later, Brookings president Michael Armacost called to talk about what we might do to help clarify the confused and conflicted relations between government and the press during national security crises. This led to a series of panels titled "The Media and the War on Terrorism," which I co-moderated with Marvin Kalb. Our first panel, "The Role of the Press: The Lessons of Wars Past," convened on October 31 with reporters who had been there: Peter Arnett, Stanley Karnow, Ted Koppel, Daniel Schorr, and the chief spokesman of the U.S. embassy in Saigon during the Vietnam War, Barry Zorthian. The third program featured a former secretary of defense, a former director of the CIA, and

a former U.S. representative to the United Nations ruminating on the media as an obstacle to getting their jobs done. In the fourth program, a former secretary of state described how he used the media to promote policies he favored. The fourteenth program, on March 27, 2002, was titled "The Impact of September 11 on Public Opinion." By the time the series ended, just after the first anniversary of 9/11, sixty-nine journalists, government officials, and scholars had examined the connections between reporting and policy. Many of the programs had been broadcast on C-SPAN; others had been broadcast around the world by the State Department. The transcripts added up to 300,000 words, which Marvin and I edited to 100,000 and published in 2003. The history of *The Media and the War on Terrorism*, as Armacost's successor, Strobe Talbott, wrote in the foreword, "underscores the special convening role that institutions like Brookings play."

Des Moines, Iowa, 1976

I instantly knew that Des Moines, Iowa, was different from Washington, D.C., when no car was waiting for me at the airport. I had come to Des Moines to work with the governor, Robert Ray, who was to be chairman of the 1976 Republican National Convention's Platform Committee. I was to be his editor in chief. What is necessary to know about Bob Ray is that when I really needed a car, he lent me his. As we worked into the night in the governor's office, I got an even better appreciation of Bob's specialness when an irate constituent called demanding that Bob get the TV station to fix whatever was interfering with that night's broadcast of Des Moines' Triple-A baseball team. As a baseball fan, I loved that to him this was not an assignment beneath a governor.

Bob Ray died in 2018, at age 89. Of his five terms as governor, according to the *New York Times*, "He embraced a fiscally responsible but progressive agenda." Most memorable to the *Washington Post* headline writer: "Iowa governor gave Vietnam War refugees a home in his state."

Kansas City, 1976

The Republican National Convention opened on August 16. The Platform Committee meetings had started the previous week. Unlike large convention cities such as New York, Los Angeles, or Chicago, the people of Kansas City were delighted to have us in town. I spent an afternoon at the Nelson-Atkins Museum of Art. (This is a country full of first-rate art museums in small cities that deserve to host political conventions if only they had more hotel rooms.) My assignment, as President Ford's representative, was to try to be obliging enough to the Reagan forces that they would not want to wage a platform fight on the convention floor. The success of this strategy emerged in Governor Reagan's remarks to the convention on August 19: "There are cynics who say that a party platform is something that no one bothers to read. . . . Whether it is different this time than it has ever been before, I believe the Republican Party has a platform that is a banner of bold, unmistakable colors with no pale pastel shades. . . . We must go forth from here united, determined and what a great general said a few years ago is true: 'There is no substitute for victory.'"

United Nations, 1974 and 1976

What can a president offer a helpful friend who is not seeking full-time employment? Our government has lots of jobs, but hardly any to reward those who are otherwise engaged. Twice President Ford offered me two- or three-month assignments that sounded intriguing. First, in 1974, I became a U.S. representative to the General Conference of the United Nations Educational, Scientific and Cultural Organization. Since the meeting place was Paris, this plum seemed especially inviting. And indeed it was for UNESCO's stuffed staff of well-paid, politically connected bureaucrats, who were led by an autocrat named Amadou-Mahtar M'Bow, said to be the worst director-general in the organization's history. The sole purpose of the United States, it was made clear to me, was to pay the bills. As I watched UNESCO repeatedly vote against our interests, including excluding Israel from a regional working group (alleging problems with its archaeological digs), Congress suspended our appropriations. I approved. I also learned not to try humor in a speech that is being simultaneously translated. Say something you think is funny, wait for the laugh as it passes through French, German, and Russian, and you will hear dead silence.

My second experience at the United Nations was as a delegate to the General Assembly, which meets from September to December each year in New York. Our standard delegation included two members of Congress (the House in odd-numbered years, the Senate in even-numbered years) and three "public members" (meaning anyone). In 1976, I was one of the anyones. Essentially, the job was to pretend to listen attentively to hundreds of speeches by heads of state. Fortunately, I sat next to the mischievous actress and singer Pearl Bailey, an honorary member of our delegation, who knitted me two wool caps while listening to the speeches. As William F. Buckley recalled, "Those of us who have served as public delegates to the United Nations are in a position to confirm that it will not matter if the president sent there J. Fred Muggs or King Timahoe to represent us." He was referring, of course, to the chimpanzee mascot of NBC's *Today* show and President Nixon's Irish setter.

My problem was that on arriving in New York, the U.S. ambassador, William Scranton, a very polite person, told me he wanted my advice! But whenever I had a suggestion, the Foreign Service professionals said "Don't rock the boat" or "That's not the way things are done." For instance, the ambassador from Saudi Arabia, Jamil Baroody, had proposed a tax on international arms purchases to underwrite the costs of the UN. Detailed study might have proved this impractical. Still, it was an innovative idea that deserved consideration. I could never get the State Department to take it seriously. I met the same indifference when I proposed that our delegation walk out of a committee meeting in which the Israelis had been prevented from presenting their side of the "occupied lands" dispute. As Senator Howard Baker, a fellow delegate, said to me,

"I feel like the boy who leaves home for the first time and his mother says, 'Write when you find work.'"

Still, there is one photo op moment that awaits the public delegate when you stand before the world assemblage to announce the U.S. position on a major issue. Even if you are only reading a piece of paper that has been handed to you, there is a tingling excitement to stand on the stage where great pronouncements have been made. The trouble was that my topic was the apartheid system in South Africa, and the U.S. position, in my opinion, was well short of articulating the outrage that the subject demanded. I made it clear that I did not like what I had been told to say, and so I started editing. Finally, I was told to stop: Secretary Kissinger had already signed off on the statement, and that was that. I changed a word or two, quite meaningless, and presented the U.S. position, along with these closing words:

> Mr. President, if I might just add one brief personal note. . . . This is in the nature of a people-to-people statement not a government-to-government one, for I'm not a professional diplomat, but rather, as is a tradition in our country, I'm a private citizen of the United States and one of three persons chosen by the President and the Senate to be a public member of our delegation. And I, too, have listened to the great debate in this Assembly for nearly a week, and from time to time I've heard an inflection in the voice of wise speakers that I've found troubling and perhaps that unease that I felt was most properly put in context by the last speaker [from Singapore] when he concluded by quoting from that inspiring novel by Alan Paton, *Cry, the Beloved Country*, when the black priest, and may I just quote those beautiful lines again, said, you will recall: "I have one great fear in my heart, that one day when they turn to loving, they will find we have turned to hating." And so, Mr. President, my personal prayer is that we may somehow seek justice in South Africa without in turn losing our sense of humanity or our capacity to love. Thank you, Mr. President.

I had no right to make this statement. Yet no one in the State Department, the United Nations, or the media said anything to me about what I said. Apparently, no one was listening.

Make-A-Wish Foundation

In 2002, I was contacted by the Make-A-Wish Foundation. The wish of a desperately ill ten-year-old boy named Daniel was to be president for a day. So when he came to Washington from Georgia with his parents and grandparents, I invited him to Brookings to be briefed by his own team of presidential advisers, all of whom had served on the staffs of other presidents. His economic adviser was Charles Schultze, his press secretary was Ron Nessen, his national security adviser was James Lindsay, and I was his speechwriter. When he returned home, we received this touching letter from his mother:

> *Dear Mr. Hess, Mr. Schultze, Mr. Lindsay, Mr. Nessen,*
> *What a pleasure it was to meet all of Daniel's Presidential Advisors! How can I thank you for making a little boy's dream to be President come true? He enjoys telling everyone that he had "real" advisors and that he learned lots of "secrets." You all are so busy to have such important work to do which made your spending time with Daniel so special. Thank you for getting down on his level and making this truly one of the highlights of his "Presidential" career. He carries the autographed book you gave him in his new briefcase that he acquired as President. While we don't know what Daniel's future holds, we do know the DC experiences will last a lifetime. . . . You have made a difference in Daniel's life and it's people like you who give him reason to keep on going . . . to keep on living . . . and to keep on believing.*
> *Fondly, Julie, "Former First Mom"*

Campaign Etiquette

When Rebecca Rimel, president of the Pew Charitable Trusts, asked Governmental Studies to do a project on political civility, I said I would see what I could figure out. I started rather mindlessly by doodling words on the computer: "advertising" . . . "bias" . . . "labels" . . . "lying" . . . "money." When I had a sufficient number of words, I arranged them alphabetically and never stopped typing. It was the easiest book I ever wrote.

The Little Book of Campaign Etiquette consisted of forty-three short essays, each concluding with a "Rule of Etiquette." For example, on labels: "Journalists should avoid ideological labels unless they take the time to define them." Or horse races: "Journalists should restrain their

Senator Moynihan gives a party at the Capitol for the
Etiquette *book. The author's family representatives include*
Eloise Levitt Hess (age three years, seven months, at left) and
Nathaniel Cody Hess (age ten and a half months, at right).

enthusiasm for horse race reporting since we will ultimately find out who wins the horse race without their help." The format was also a natural for including the work of some of my favorite political cartoonists, such as a Jeff MacNelly panel in the *Chicago Tribune* that shows a candidate speaking into a telephone: "Uh . . . What do the polls say my core beliefs are?" Or a Clay Bennett cartoon in the *Christian Science Monitor* of a TV newsman saying to the candidate, "Political campaigns have become so simplistic and superficial. . . . In the 20 seconds we have left, could you explain why?"

What the book needed was a fitting introduction. So I asked Judith Martin, the famous "Miss Manners." She told me that her parents had met through Brookings. (It had to do with two economists, one of whom had a sister. . . .) And therefore she felt obligated to accept the assignment, which began: "It is an honor, not to mention a mercy, to welcome Stephen Hess to the noble profession of telling people to cut that out right this minute if they know what's good for them and start behaving like civilized human beings."

The book that I did not know I wanted to write won the National Press Club's Award for Press Criticism in 1999 and also a note from Rebecca Rimel: "The book's sobering message, overlaid with wry, and at times poignant humor, hits just the right note in today's political climate." Brookings published another edition for the 2000 presidential election.

Political Cartoons

When I went to the Library of Congress in 1959 looking for a few political cartoons to add bulk to my first book, I never imagined that in 1998 I would be the opening speaker at a conference on the state of political cartooning, where I confessed to "an almost forty-year love affair with American political cartooning."

One thing leads to another. My book on American political cartoons, co-authored with Milton Kaplan, was published in 1968 under the gender-offensive title, *The Ungentlemanly Art*. We revised it in 1975 to capture the cartoonists' takes on Watergate, including Garry Trudeau's 1973 *Doonesbury* strip declaring former attorney general John Mitchell "Guilty, Guilty, Guilty!"

In the mid-1990s, public television producer Sandy Northrop was planning a PBS series on the history of American political cartoons. The films did not happen, but the book did: *Drawn & Quartered*, a coffee-table book originally planned as a companion to the series, was published in 1996. Our friendship produced a second book, *American Political Cartoons: The Evolution of a National Identity, 1754–2010,* as well as two three-minute segments for PBS's *NewsHour* that traced the 2004 presidential contest through the work of the cartoonists. As a bonus, twice I was a Pulitzer juror for the editorial cartooning prize, in 1989 and 1990, where, unsuccessfully, I tried to promote cartoons whose targets were mayors rather than Ho Chi Minh. I was also an expert witness in a case in which a little environmental newsletter was sued by a giant utilities company that held the trademark on a happy little figure made up of sparks and sockets and light bulbs. The utilities were not pleased with how the newsletter's cartoons depicted their stick figure. My role was to recount the history of symbols in cartooning. "Your Honor, if the swastika could not have been used by cartoonists because it's the trademark of the American Nazi Party or the hooded figure the trademark of the Ku Klux Klan. . . ."

I had some really good stuff ready to deliver, but when I got on the stand Howard Corcoran, judge for the U.S. District Court for the District of Columbia, called my views "esoterica." "What's political cartooning got to do with this case?" asked Judge Corcoran. The newsletter won the case when the judge ruled the utilities company had not legally protected its trademark.

There seemed to be no end to where political cartooning popped up in my life. In Istanbul I spent a fascinating morning with Turkish newspaper cartoonists whose artistry equaled the best in the United States. Perhaps the lower a country's literacy, the more the artists have to reach beyond tags and captions to win their audience. In Beijing, when I was invited by the Chinese Academy of Social Science to address a conference on tradition, what better than to use America's history of political cartooning to illustrate freedom of speech?

The Notorious RBG

When Marty Ginsburg, the distinguished law professor at Georgetown, called me on April 14, 1993, it was to talk about his wife Ruth's prospects for the seat that was about to become available on the U.S. Supreme Court. An excellent idea! Calling me was sensible, too, since I was the only politician in the family. Ruth—in the family she is Kiki—was my wife's first cousin: Ruth's mother and Beth's father were sister and brother. If Marty had asked about a regulatory commission, I could have given a textbook answer. But the Supreme Court was a puzzlement. I knew of no standard path from here to there. It was a question that I devoted much thought to over the next two months. There was hardly a day that Marty and I did not review the bidding. What does important Washington lawyer William Coleman think? This was the sort of question we asked each other. The hours I spent lobbying for Ruth's nomination I took as annual leave from my day job at Brookings.

What is stunning to remember when looking back at what now seems obvious is that there were four candidates before Ruth from whom President Clinton was prepared to choose. First was Richard Arnold, a U.S. Court of Appeals judge in Little Rock and a close friend of the president. He had cancer and would die the next year. Then Bruce Babbitt, the secretary of the interior, whom the conservation community emphatically did not want Clinton to take from them. Third was Mario Cuomo, the former New York governor, who told the president he did not want the job. Fourth was Stephen Breyer, who was not in great shape from a bicycle accident when he met the president and would have to wait a little longer. Then Ruth.

My biggest contribution to Ruth's eventual nomination was in convincing Pat Moynihan to champion her selection. Later, Ruth thanked

Senator Moynihan from the White House Rose Garden for "special caring," adding "I do not actually know [him]." But he was my best friend and Ruth would become our cause. There was a third person on our team—Robert Katzmann, Pat's teaching assistant at Harvard and later my colleague at Brookings, who was to guide Ruth through her Senate introductions. Pat's logs show that on Thursday, June 10, I told him about Harvard Law School dean Erwin Griswold's 1985 speech in which he said that America's two greatest litigators were Thurgood Marshall and Ruth Bader Ginsburg. This was an amazing piece of evidence! The next day I gave Pat the citation for the Griswold quote, and on June 11 he sent the transcript to David Gergen at the White House. As chairman of the Senate Finance Committee, Pat had instant access to the White House—not the case with every senator. Marty led a drumbeat of endorsements to keep Ruth's name in contention until the president could make up his mind. This was our "inside strategy"—in that we kept away from the media and did not challenge the qualifications of rival candidates.

On Sunday, June 13, the president made his decision. When he called Pat at midnight to tell him he would announce Ruth's nomination the next day, Pat immediately called me, and I immediately called Ruth, who said she had not called me because she knew we did not like to take calls after ten o'clock. We talked until two in the morning about what she would say at the White House. She was magnificent.

It was a treat to be a close observer of Ruth's remarkable career. And during national elections she even gave me a role of sorts. This was because Chief Justice William Rehnquist loved to bet. According to the delightful biography *Rehnquist* by his friend Herman (Obi) Obermayer, "He would bet on almost anything: how much snow would fall in the Supreme Court's courtyard on a particular morning, which football team would next sack the quarterback. The point spread between top contestants in a California primary election." Thus, by direction of the chief justice, the eight associate justices followed him into an "election pool" of his design in even-numbered years. There was Pool A ($5.00 per person), with 50 percent of the winnings going to the justice with the most correct picks, 30 percent for the second most correct picks, and 20 percent for the third most. Pool B ($3.00 per person) was for the net gain or loss for Republicans in the House, and Pool C (also $3.00) was for the net gain or loss for Republicans in the Senate. Obi, who was also my friend, explained that Rehnquist had "his own special sub rosa political intelligence organization" made up of his former law clerks, who reported from their home states on the latest election prospects. But poor Ruth had only me. With her permission, her handwritten note of November 14, 1996, reads "Dear Steve, IOU 65¢ & appreciation for placing me with the winners." Two years later, 1998, the note was now typed: "Dear Steve: Sad to report, I lost $2.16 to Steve Breyer. Still, I did better than the Chief, who owes Steve $5.50. Next year, I will consult you and Beth." Next year the court made history in *Bush v. Gore.*

Another small story: On a Friday evening in 1996 at 10:30 p.m., Ruth called. She apologized because it was after ten. She had received a letter full of misspellings announcing that an unknown-to-her foundation was giving her $100,000, no strings attached. She needed counsel. I said we were coming over for dinner tomorrow anyway and I knew a person on the committee and would see what I could find out. The foundation, it turned out, was one rich man who wanted to honor someone every year, without publicity. I suggested she had three choices: she could keep the money (no), she could return the money (no), or she could give the money away. But how? My thought was that she ask ten dear friends to each pick a charity or organization to receive a check from the foundation. She liked the idea. Beth and I directed our $10,000 "Ginsburg grant" to a pediatric hospice program.

Hyman Rickover, "Father of the Nuclear Navy," 1954

I was a twenty-two-year-old student with an afternoon job on the staff of the mayor of Baltimore's Commission on Mass Transportation. The chairman was the Johns Hopkins professor Abel Wolman, the pioneer of

11/14/96

Dear Steve

65¢

+ appreciation
me with th
Drawn &
last nigh

November 6, 1998

Stephen Hess
3705 Porter Street, N.W.
Washington, D.C. 20016

Dear Steve:

Sad to report, I lost $2.16 to Steve Breyer. Still, I did better than the Chief, who owes Steve $5.50. Next year, I will consult you and Beth.

Love to you,

Kiki

Ruth Bader Ginsburg

modern sanitary engineering. He was a deliberate and reasoned person, and I was stunned when he informed me that he had told his friend Hyman Rickover that I was the writer to do the secret history of *Nautilus*, Rickover's amazing achievement—the world's first nuclear-powered vessel. Truly, I had never spoken with Dr. Wolman about my future. Yet he must have known something I did not know. He sent me to Washington, where Admiral Rickover was housed in the Main Navy Building, a "temporary" structure built on the National Mall in 1918 for military offices. Sitting behind his desk, the admiral looked to me like an artist's rendering for the cover of *Time*, in what I thought of as complexion sallow, tint green.

He did not waste words. "No, I want Morison!" Meaning Samuel Eliot Morison, author of the fifteen-volume history of the Navy in World War II.

That was all he said to me, other than thanking me for coming. Still, I had met a great—if strange—man, and I had a story to tell. All in all, not a bad afternoon.

Jacqueline Kennedy Onassis, 1977

The Institute of Politics at Harvard's John F. Kennedy School of Government was having its tenth anniversary celebration on a Saturday in late April: a series of panel discussions in the morning, a picnic in the afternoon, and a dinner and dance in the evening. I agreed to moderate a panel on the parties. The itinerary was at the hotel when I arrived: The panel was to meet in the Junior Common Room of Leverett House from ten to noon. The ten participants were a well-balanced group and included Republican Lamar Alexander, soon to be governor of Tennessee; Democrat Philip Hoff, former governor of Vermont; David Keene, future chairman of the American Conservative Union; the liberal congressman Allard Lowenstein; and . . . Jacqueline Kennedy Onassis, editor. A panicked call to the institute's director, Jonathan Moore: What are you doing to me? He replied, not to be questioned: Every member of the senior advisory committee is put on a panel and Jackie is your member.

Leverett House was stuffed with spectators. The other panel rooms must have been uninhabited as a result of Jackie's scheduled appearance here. Yet by ten o'clock, Mrs. Onassis had not arrived. Nevertheless, I started the program and gave each panelist the opportunity to make a statement. After about twenty-five minutes she entered. I welcomed her, got her seated in the empty chair at the end of the row, and said, "Since you have not had the opportunity to hear the other speakers, it would be unfair to ask you to speak now." She nodded politely. It was a lively discussion—yet Jackie had not said anything. At noon I turned to her.

"Mrs. Onassis, you are the only editor on our panel. You have heard the conversation. My question is: Would you give us a contract?"

"Yes!" she replied, in her famous willowy voice. She seemed pleased with her response.

The audience burst into applause. I thanked the participants and concluded the program.

That night I asked Jackie to dance. She told me with emotion how frightened she had been and how grateful she was to me. I had been worrying for myself. How much more terrifying it must have been for her. We never met again. Nor could I have asked her to recount that experience. But what an amazing act of strength it was for her to walk into that room.

Richard Avedon, 1990

Pat and Liz Moynihan were giving a cocktail party in their Capitol Hill home to honor their daughter's engagement to Richard Avedon's son. I was early; the only other guest present was Richard Avedon himself. An unexpected chance for a few words more than "nice to meet you." Still, what to say to the great photographer? Since I did not even own a camera, my ignorance limited my questions, which he did not seem to mind. When I asked about his archival plans, he told me he was giving his negatives to Arizona State University in Tucson. Then he said something odd: he was drawing an X through each frame. Surely, I wondered, there was not a less intrusive way to preserve. . . . But our conversation went no further as other guests arrived and wanted his attention.

At nine the next morning, the telephone rang in my office. "This is Dick Avedon. You asked a good question last night and I didn't give you a proper answer." What a startling call! He did not know me. He must have asked the Moynihans for my number. He explained the difference between news photography and his type of work, how the printing of the photograph ultimately defined the difference. The X indicated that that frame could never be reproduced as an "Avedon." Years later I read an article in the *New York Times* about a disagreement over the process of printing his work: "A single exhibition print might take 45 minutes, with each part of a face or item of clothing receiving its own dose of timed light."

Oliver Stone, 1994

My wife and I were in Los Angeles visiting grandchildren when my daughter-in-law, the casting director Heidi Levitt, asked if I would talk to Oliver Stone, who was then planning a movie about Richard Nixon. She set up a meeting in his Santa Monica office. Stone was not particularly animated, and our conversation probably lasted no more than half an hour. But as I was leaving I asked if he had known that Nixon was in Dallas on November 22, 1963.

His eyes widened: "Was he on the grassy knoll?"

He asked to stay in touch, and eventually I arranged a working lunch for us in a private dining room at Brookings. He brought Anthony Hopkins (who would play Nixon), James Woods (Bob Haldeman), and his researcher, Eric Hamburg. On the other side of the table were four people who might help them better understand Nixon—former press secretary Ron Ziegler, Nixon's law partner Len Garment, political aide John Sears, and myself. At some point I whispered to Hopkins, who had told me to call him Tony: "Listen, Tony, each one of us is describing a totally different person!" Could this be of use? After lunch I invited Oliver and Tony and Jim, our new friends, to go upstairs to Governance Studies and talk movies with the staff. I think they enjoyed themselves. We certainly enjoyed them. Everything was "off the record," which meant that the paparazzi were outside Brookings waiting for them.

Former British Prime Minister John Major, 2009

The scene was straight out of *Downton Abbey*. We were at Ditchley Park in Oxfordshire. Elizabeth I had visited the Ditchley estate in 1592, annoyed that its owner, Sir Henry Lee, had married one of her ladies-in-waiting without her permission. So she deliberately stayed too long, thus costing Sir Henry a great deal of money. Or so the story goes. The present Ditchley Park was built in 1722 and evolved through various owners with titles like the fourth earl of this or the seventeenth viscount of that, until it was sold to a rich Anglo-American, Ronald Tree, in 1932.

This worked well for history because Ronald Tree was of Winston Churchill's set, and during World War II, when Churchill was advised not to go to Chequers, the prime minister's official country residence, he spent weekends at Ditchley. In 1958, then-owner Sir David Wills donated the mansion and its 280 acres of parkland to the Ditchley Foundation, where U.K.-U.S. conferences are held. The one that Beth and I attended in 2009 was titled "Managing the Machinery of Government in Periods of Change."

At the first dinner, I was directed to be seated next to the former prime minister John Major. This caused me to say too loud, "What will I ever talk about with the prime minister?" Fortunately, a man behind me—I think it was the Right Honourable Lord Butler—said, "Talk about music halls."

"Why music halls?"

"Because his father managed one and he is writing a book about it."

Following standard introductions, I politely inquired, "Sir, may I ask how your book on music halls is coming?"

He was startled. "How did you know?"

"We have our sources," I replied.

We laughed. My spy talk answer was so ridiculous. His book, *My Old Man*, is generous and warm-hearted, I am told. We have our sources.

Beth also made a friend, the Right Honourable Christopher Geidt, private secretary to Her Majesty the Queen. She told me they talked about Alan Bennett's delightful novella, *The Uncommon Reader*, the story of Elizabeth II following her corgi into a mobile library for the kitchen staff at Buckingham Palace. Too polite to leave without borrowing a book, she becomes obsessed with literature, thereby changing the country's culture.

Circles within Circles

My Brookings life evolved into concentric circles of research, travel, advising, writing, talking, teaching. Did everything relate to everything else? Sort of.

The most fun I had in the classroom was challenging my students on whether they could tell if an article had been written by a man or a woman. This was a by-product of what the *New York Times* had called "arguably the first sex scandal in corporate America." Mary Cunningham graduated from Harvard Business School in 1979, at the age of twenty-seven, then in 1980 went to work for the Bendix Company, whose president, William Agee, kept promoting her beyond traditional expectations. Cunningham was always described in the press as "strawberry blonde" or by some other alluring feature. However, one day a *Wall Street Journal* column noted the attractiveness of Agee. Was this written by a woman? It was! So I took four articles—one from the *Wall Street Journal*, one from the *New York Times*, and two from the *Washington Post*—cut off the bylines, and asked my Harvard graduate students to guess the gender of the reporter. My elite class—seven women and five men—included a state senator, a university administrator, a consumer advocate, and several government officials.

The group voted nine to three that the *Wall Street Journal* reporter was a man. (She was a woman.) Eleven of the twelve students thought the *New York Times* reporter was a woman. (He was a man.) They were wrong on both *Washington Post* articles. There was no article on which a majority of the students got the right answer, no student got more than half right, and three students got them all wrong. Collectively the class received a grade of 29 percent. The men and women earned equally low marks. A friend gave my test to his students at Syracuse University and got similar results. This produced some excellent discussion. Perhaps looking at four articles in newspapers of high professional standing did not prove anything. But I think it did!

For several years in the late 1970s and through the 1980s, every third week I wrote a newspaper column that ran in about thirty-five cities around the country. I thought of it as a sort of breakfast reading, "Government 101." Among the columns were "Government Reorganization, What It Can and Cannot Do," "The Loss of Privacy in America," "Can the Republicans Get Their Act Together?," "In Defense of Politicians," "When a President's Popularity Declines, 'Don't Just Stand There—Do Something,'" "How Government Creates Problems," and "The Law of Unanticipated Consequences." There was one column dedicated to "good news," in which an exasperated President Nixon asked his secretary of state, William P. Rogers, "Isn't there any good news?" To which Rogers, after consulting his notes, replied, "Mr. President, I can report that there's a crack in the Aswan Dam." If only my ideas were endless! Sadly, they were not. After about a hundred columns, I could see I was on the verge of repeating myself, so I ended the column.

There was a trip to Jos in the highlands of Nigeria when the generals wanted to discuss what form of government best fitted their country's needs. Parliamentary—simpler than the American mode, I urged. No, they insisted, they hated the British too much and preferred to think that their tribes were like our states. The president-elect of Colombia wanted help organizing his executive office. We met secretly in Orlando because his children wanted to see Disney World. I tutored the wonderful Anna Devere Smith on the culture of Washington for a play she was writing. At a conference in Sochi, on the coast of the Black Sea, we talked about newspaper journalism in Russia. At a conference in Thessaloniki, we talked about television in Greece. For a graduate course on the presidency at the University of Southern California in Los Angeles, I shoehorned a semester into ten days by taping my interviews, cutting them into sections—like congressional relations and speechwriting—and bringing the "lecturers" with me. I lectured at Mishkenot Sha'ananim, in Jerusalem, overlooking the walls of the Old City directly across from Mount Zion. Jeane Kirkpatrick and I debated Cornel West and Roberto Unger on election reform. I met with a Swedish delegation to examine the possibilities of the country starting its own C-SPAN. I met with Brazilians to review plans for a presidential election transition. With Kathryn Dunn Tenpas, I studied White House turnover rates in 2001, a project she continues. I found excuses to say I had slept at least one night in all fifty states, which always started a conversation. In Helsinki, I represented the United States at a five-nation conference on the Future of Transatlantic Relations.

And in 2004, I became senior fellow emeritus at Brookings, where I still keep my office, adding another office for five years when President Stephen Trachtenberg of George Washington University invited me to be distinguished research professor of media and public affairs. It was where I learned what parts of academic novels are accurate.

———————

In 1958, I rushed into national politics, grateful for the unexpected opportunities and ultimately thinking I had learned some useful things about how government works. Could there be a mid-career correction? Fortunately, I had made enough money to give myself a little space to turn around. Choosing bookmaking as the avenue out of politics was a risky strategy. Count the successes. It required some mix of self-confidence and arrogance. Luck too. But "Public Person," if that is what I wanted to become, is not in the *Dictionary of Occupational Titles* anyway. A senior fellow at the Brookings Institution must have sounded like a strange ambition. In 1972, when my professional life turned, Brookings too was in the process of changing. And I fit much of what Kermit Gordon and

Gilbert Steiner were looking for. My books, which academics would not read when I asked to chair the government's humanities program, were essentially the types of books that Brookings would make the foundation of public policy schools. Some government service was a plus, not a liability. Although the matter was left unspoken, Kermit's raids on personnel from the Kennedy and Johnson administrations probably made my being a Republican an asset. Sometimes you deeply want something to happen—and it happens!

That's it for now at eighty-five. Beth, what did I leave out?

Spring training. Hess opens another season as a legendary fan. Sons Charles and James outfit the Brookings righthander at cleanup after Jayson Werth.

Afterword

Two thousand sixteen was an election year that I would have preferred not to notice. Impossible, of course, and on February 15, Jill Lawrence gave me enough space in *USA Today* to express my concern, headlined: "Trump Has No Idea How to Be President: Stephen Hess," with the subheading *"What amazes me is his total lack of interest in trying to understand the presidency."*

This was personal. I had been there and had spent my life trying to find ways to make the institution work better.

In August, after his nomination, I tried again. This time my plea was directed at Republicans. My op-ed appeared in *Newsweek*, the title spread across the page in capital letters:

I Served Ike, Nixon, Ford and Reagan. But I Can't Vote Donald Trump.

My statement read, in part: "Donald Trump will lose the election just as soon as millions of other Republicans like me recognize that there has never been a major party candidate as profoundly ignorant of the presidency or of what goes into being president."

On January 20, 2017, I was in a TV studio to do live TV commentary of the inaugural address. I had done this many times. It is my favorite presidency moment. Symbolically the candidate casts off campaign-speak and seeks words to unite and bind the nation. At best this will be a speech of grace and elegance: Lincoln's First and Second; FDR's "the only thing we have to fear is fear itself"; Jack Kennedy telling us to "ask not what your country can do for you." Instead the new president delivered a populist shout-out about "American carnage." I was shocked. "From this day forward, it's going to be only America first—America first."

I made an important decision, tough, strange given my history. I was not going to answer reporters' questions about the president. Each "quote," in the Washington habit of sourcing, would only lead to another quote and then another. I would gladly watch others, sometimes with a tinge of envy, say what I might have said when I was younger. I was determined not to engage in constant conflict.

In a busy life, suddenly there was space to try something new.

Fred Dews, the host of Brookings Cafeteria Podcast, lured me into his studio to hear me tell stories. He is a skilled interviewer, and it was fun.

My view of memoir writing, however, was expressed by the Victoria Roberts cartoon in the *New Yorker:* two turtles, one saying to the other in her or his shell: "Whatever you do in there all day is fine with me, so long as it's not writing a memoir."

I was of the old school in thinking that one has to be very important—at least a general in a serious war—to presume to write a memoir. Henry Aaron, my Brookings colleague, I think was the person to convince me that there are more of us than there are of them, and therefore the experiences of the bit player may be more useful to more people. Maybe. But did I really need an excuse? Beth told me to read Robert Butler's theory of reminiscence. The past months have been a joy of learning and remembering as I have tried to recreate the arc of my working life.

Thanks

Anyone who has read this far knows that the author has a lot to be thankful for, and hence a lot of people to thank.

Governance Studies has been my home at Brookings for almost exactly half my life. Beyond its leadership—from directors Gil Steiner through Darrell West—and its scholars, what I deeply appreciate are the people in the offices next to the director and at the welcoming desk. Yes, they make the trains run on time (if this were a railroad rather than a think tank), but what I will always remember is that they like me, which I return! This is not irrelevant: if you have ever worked in a large organization, you'll understand. The GS annual budget is over $10 million.

Thank you, dear Donna Verdier, Diane Hodges, Vida Megahed, Eloise Stinger, Sandra Riegler, Susan Stewart, Renuka Deonarain, Cynthia Terrels, Radmila Nikolic, Bob Brier, Pat Fowlkes, Liz Valentini, Anna Goodbaum, Beth Stone, and Hillary Schaub. It has been more than twenty years since Pat left GS, yet we still try to lunch twice a year so I can fight her for the check. My wife and I exchange long holiday letters with Diane to catch up on her life in Chicago. I assume the same will be true now that Hillary is in Philadelphia. The offices they once occupied are now staffed by Emily Perkins, Liz Sablich, and a new crew.

There are so many to appreciate: the people who can locate any book anywhere with such grace, Laura Mooney and Sarah Chilton, and the calm-voiced authorities at the end of the IT help line.

Another category of special and talented people is populated by a generation of my research assistants: Ethan Basch, Julie Connor, Buck Ratchford, Fawn Johnson, Deborah Kalb, Andrew Cowan, Daniel Reilly, and Jessica Garrity. They are now lawyers, writers, professors, even a doctor of massive achievements (who had to decide whether he should go to medical school or compose musical comedies when he worked for me).

I also love being surrounded by each term's invasion of college interns, so proud to be working at Brookings. And no, they don't all come from Harvard, Yale, or Stanford. My representative bunch in 1985–86, for instance, came from Cornell, St. Lawrence, Rochester, Georgetown, Vermont, Middlebury, Connecticut College—and one from Harvard. Gene Sperling from the University of Minnesota literally knocked on my door, and I said, "Sure, I can always use another." Some do very well post-Brookings. (Gene is one of my three interns who made it into a president's cabinet.) Years later I met again Janet Hatfield (St. Lawrence), now the Reverend Janet Hatfield Legro of St. Paul's Memorial Church at the University of Virginia. She claims she became what she is because I steered her away from political science. What will be the future of my *Bit Player* intern, Ananya Hanhavan, who now returns to Wellesley College?

The other behind-the-curtain people to whom I owe so much are my editors. I claim authorship of twenty-four books, but counting can be a question because if a book goes into three editions, with the third edition very different from first, should it be counted as one book or two? In this case I counted all editions as one. In a somewhat similar case in which the title changed, I counted two. Six of the books were published by major commercial presses: these were my earliest efforts, and from those presses—with gratitude—I had the most to learn: Random House, 1960: Jess Stein and Charles Lieber; Doubleday, 1966: Ellin K. Roberts; Harper & Row, 1967: Jeannette Hopkins; Macmillan, 1968: Peter V. Ritner and Herbert Rosenthal (designer). A later book was published in 2011 by Transaction at Rutgers, run by the formidable Irving Louis Horowitz.

Of the seventeen books published by Brookings Institution Press, ten were edited by James R. Schneider. We thought of ourselves as a team. What better than having an editor who knows exactly what to worry about before you do? "Don't you think chapter 5 fits better before chapter 3?" When Jim died, I was inherited by Eileen Hughes, and we worked seamlessly on three books. When she retired, Brookings contracted for editor Richard Walker, now at the U.S. Institute of Peace. It was a decision made in editorial heaven by managing editor Janet Walker, who was so skilled at these sorts of things. Richard and I have now done three books together, including *Bit Player*.

When the manuscript leaves Richard we know what the book is meant to be. It then goes to Marjorie Pannell for line-to-line approval.

They are my links to how I want to be remembered, based on judgments big and little.

Examples of two recent editorial decisions:

- A Richard Walker decision: Delete the paragraph on the Nixon White House football team. I thought it was funny. The editor thought it was too slight. Bruce Ladd, who had been the team's manager, will be sad. Perhaps I can use it someplace sometime.

- A Marjorie Pannell decision: "Because of the dangling participles," she emails, "I would suggest a full stop after 'spectacular.' Then: 'Angling across a gated street. . . .'" Marjorie is right; the change will be made.

Two others we must then turn to are proofreader Carlotta Ribar and indexer Sherry L. Smith.

Brookings still cares about books, while, it seems to me, the end product of many other think tanks is reports. Books simply require a lot of caring, which has required leadership during my years here of directors Bob Faherty, Valentina Kalk, and now Bill Finan and Yelba Quinn. When I told Valentina that I might write a memoir, she gave me her favorite memoir as a gift. There is the need too for production people, such as the talented Elliott Beard, who designed and typeset this book's pages.

Finally, there are decisions about a book's cover. The cover design for *Bit Player* was suggested by my son, Charles Hess. I tell him I don't want representational—no White House, no presidents; strong graphics will be fine. His response: No, it's a memoir, and the cover should be a portrait of the memoirist. Charlie, this is a Brookings book; Putin might be the only person whose portrait is allowed on the cover on a Brookings book! Bill Finan agrees with the designer, overrules the author. Charlie knows just the right artist, Lori Mehta in Boston.

The cover arrives. I love it.

Thanks, there is now a book.

Index

Aaron, Henry, 124, 126, 180
ABC television, 64, 144
Adams, John, 116
Adams, John Quincy, 116
Adams, Sherman, 3, 16–17, 19, 23
AFL-CIO, Massachusetts, 100
Agee, William, 174
Agnew, Spiro T., 68, 89–95
Ailes, Roger, 66
Akihito, Crown Prince, 28
Alaska cruise, 155, *157*
Albright, Madeleine, 149
Alcorn, Mead, 4
Alexander, Clifford, *9,* 10
Alexander, Lamar, 100, 170
Ambassadorship offers, Hess's, 110,
    116
American Council of Learned Soci-
    eties, 117

American Political Cartoons (Hess
    and Northrup), 165
American Political Dynasties (Hess),
    18, 76, 78–80
Anderson, Jack, 104–05
Anderson, John, 137–38
Anderson, Robert B., 32
Angels in the Outfield (movie), 20–21
Antiwar movement, 83, 103, 109,
    112
Apartheid statement, UN assembly,
    161–62
Arden House, 131
Areeda, Phil, 27
Arizona State University, 171–72
Armacost, Michael, 156
Arnett, Peter, 156
Arnold, Richard, 166
Arthur, Chester, 46–47

Article writing, Hess's. *See* Writing projects, Hess's
Aspin, Les, 146
The Atlantic, 139
Aurand, Pete, 21
Avedon, Richard, 171–72
Avery, Mr., 41

Babbitt, Bruce, 166
Bailey, Pearl, 160
Baker, Howard, 160–61
Baltimore, Republican Party, 13–14
Baltimore Evening News, 16
Baltimore Evening Sun, 91–92
Baltimore Sun, 36, 40–41, 93
Baroody, Jamil, 160
Barry, Dave, 123
Barry, Marion, 136
Baseball, 7
Beach, Edward L. "Ned," 24–25
Beard question, 136
Beer, Sam, 126
Begnoche, Michelle, 144
Bell, Alphonzo, 79
Bell, Jack, 32
Bellagio Study and Conference Center, 144
Bendix Company, 174
Ben-Gurion, David, 67
Bennett, Alan, 174
Bennett, Clay, 164
Benson, Ezra Taft, 19, 45–46
Berlin, Irving, 12
Berman, Ronald S., 118
Bigart, Homer, 91
The Biographical Directory of the
United States Congress, 18
Bit player, defined, 106
Black Man in the White House (Morrow), 27
Blough, Roger, 74
Blumenthal, Richard, 98, 100
Board of Education, District of Columbia, 129
Bookmaking topics, Hess's: with Brookings opportunity, 176–77; campaign etiquette, 163–64; home office for, 75–76; Moynihan, 95, 101; news media, 140–46, 158; Nixon, 77, *78,* 87, 88, 95, 101; political cartoons, 76, 164–65; political dynasties, 18, 76, 78–80; presidency organization, 138–39; presidential campaigns, 128–29; presidential candidates, 14, 76, 88; presidential transitions, 151; Republican Party, 61, 76–77, 83. *See also* Writing projects, Hess's
Book-of-the-Month Club, 138
Born Again (Colson), 134
Boston Globe, 79
Bosworth, Barry, 126
Bragdon, John, 25
Brazil, presidential transition planning, 176
Breyer, Stephen, 27, 166, 168
Bricker Amendment, 5–6
Brikner, Michael, 44
British parliamentarians, during September 11 attacks, 156
Brock, Bill, 148

Broder, David, 61, 77, 80
Brookings, Robert S., 123
Brookings Cafeteria Podcast, 180
Brookings Institution, Hess's
    position: conference gatherings,
    130–31; as good fit, 176–77;
    Governmental Studies program,
    126–29; listing of activities, 175–
    76; news interviews, 135–37;
    presidential transition studies,
    150; recruitment process, 124,
    126; and September 11 attacks,
    156, 158. *See also* Bookmaking
    topics, Hess's; Writing projects,
    Hess's
Brookings Institution, history over-
    view, 123–24
Brookings Institution Press, 129
*Brookings Papers on Economic Activ-
    ity,* 126
Brown, Jerry, 10
Brown, Pat, 60, 61, 68–69, 70, 71,
    82
Brown v. Board of Education, 43
Brzezinski, Zbigniew, 150
Buchanan, Pat, 59, 81, 94, 117, 134
Buckley, William F., 160
Bumiller, Elisabeth, 142
Burkhardt, Frederick, 117
Burns, Arthur, 34, 101, 134
Burtless, Gary, 126
Bush, George H. W., 149
Bush, George W., 143, 144, 150
Butler, Lord, 173
Butler, Robert, 180
Butterfield, Alexander, 135

California Energy Commission, 10
Calkins, Robert, 124
Campaign Award, 143
Carnegie Endowment for Interna-
    tional Peace, 149
Carter, Jimmy, 52, 139, 147–48,
    150, 151
CBS News, 142
Center for Technology Innovation,
    Brookings Institution, 128
Central Intelligence Agency, 21
Champion, Hale, 82
Champion, Marge, 108
Cheney, Dick, 139, 148
Chermayeff, Ivan, 105
Chesney, Earle, 26
Chicago, vote fraud accusation, 87
Chicago Sun-Times, 88, 94
Chicago Tribune, 87, 164
Chiesa, Vivian della, 80
Childhood/youth, Hess's, 6–10
China, political cartoon talk, 165–66
Choice, 79
Christian Science Monitor, 16, 164
Christopher, George, 61
Churchill, Winston, 173
City Council, District of Columbia,
    130
Civility book, campaign, 163–64
Civil rights policies, Eisenhower's,
    43
Clark, Joseph, 127
Clinton, Bill, 6, 149–50, 151,
    166–67
CNN, 137–38
Cohen, Mr., 99

Coit, Margaret, 79

Coleman, William, 166

College years, Hess's, 5–6, 10–13

Colombia, 175

Colson, Chuck, 134

Columbia Journalism Review, 140

Columbia University, 11, 131

Commission on Mass Transportation, Baltimore, 168, 170

Compact of Fifth Avenue, 30

Congress, U.S., 37, 40–41, 45–46, 160. *See also* Senate, U.S.

Congressional Budget Office, 126

Congressional Record, 5, 43

Connors, Chuck, 66

Coolidge, Calvin, 20, 24

Cooper, John Sherman, 31

Corcoran, Howard, 165

Cox, Archibald, 136

Cronkite, Walter, 12

Crossfire, 137

Crossword puzzle clue, 125

Cry, the Beloved Country (Paton), 161

Cuban missile crisis, 68, 70–71

Cunningham, Mary, 174

Cuomo, Mario, 166

Dallas Morning News, 74

Daniel, president-for-a-day, 162

Danzansky, Stephen, 110–11

Dean, John, 105, 135

Democratic National Committee, 131

Democratic Party, 6, 53, 61. *See also* Carter, Jimmy; Kennedy, John F. (and administration)

DeMuth, Christopher, 98

Derthick, Martha, 127

Desegregation policies, Eisenhower's, 43

Des Moines, Iowa, 158

Dewey, Tom, 12, 25, 74

Dews, Fred, 180

Dillon, Douglas, 51

"Dinner with Ike" speech, 41–42

Dionne, E. J., Jr., 77, 142

Dirksen, Everett McKinley, 12, 67

District of Columbia, governance, 129–30

Ditchley Park, 173

Dole, Elizabeth, 100

Doonesbury comic strip, 165

Doubleday, 73

Draft abolishment idea, 83, 112

Draper, William G., 33–34

Drawn & Quartered (Hess), 165

Drucker, Peter, 138

Duke Law School, 58

Dulles, John Foster, 19

Duncan, Todd, 28

Dunham, Katherine, 108

Economic Studies program, Brookings Institution, 126

Education organizations, District of Columbia, 129–30

Edwards, James, 146

Ego Leak, 142

Ehrlichman, John, 98, 101, 110, 117, 118

Eisenhower, David, 83–85

Eisenhower, Dwight D. (and administration): attacks from John Birch Society, 62; congressional elections speechmaking, 37, 40–41; Fort Ligonier speech, 4–5; and Kennedy administration transition, 147; and Kennedy assassination, 74; leisure activities, 20–21; and Nixon's campaigns, 33, 34–35, 69–70, 87; nominations of, 11–12, 85; perspective on vice presidency, 57–58; platform drafting support, 28, 30–31; post-presidency correspondence, 53–57; press conference about VP's role, 31–33; reminiscences about, 44–47; social events, 22–23, 28, *29*; speechwriting processes, 35–39, 41–43, 58–59; staff operations described, 3–4, 21–22, 23–28, 51

Eisenhower, John, 24, 32, 57
Eisenhower, Mamie, 20, 34, 35, 87
Eisenhower, Milton, 26, 36
Electoral College discussions, 131
Elizabeth I, 173
Elizabeth II, 22, 174
Ellsberg, Daniel, 135
Encounters with Eisenhower, 44
England, 22, 173, 174
Estes Park, White House Youth Conference, 111–13
Ethical Culture School, 8
Europe trip, Hess's, 11
Evans, Rowland, 91
Executive Office Building, 19

Fallows, James, 139
Family Assistance Plan, Nixon administration, 101, 128
Family background, Hess's, 6–8
Farewell Address, Eisenhower's, 37, 43, 46
Federal City College, District of Columbia, 129
Fellow position at Harvard, Hess's, 82. *See also* Brookings Institution, Hess's position
Fields, W. C., 14
Fieldston News, 9, 10
Fieldston school, 8–10
Film narration, Republican platform, 28, 31
Finch, Bob, 69, 102, 110
Finn, Chester "Checker," 98
Fish Room, White House, 21
Flanigan, Peter, 116
Fleming, Rhonda, 66
Flemming, Arthur, 26
Flood, Daniel, 104
Folger, Cliff, 75
Fonda, Jane, 88
Football Hall of Fame Dinner, 39
Ford, Gerald, 67, 136, 138–39, 148, 159
Foreign Policy Studies program, Brookings Institution, 126
Fort Ligonier speech, Eisenhower's, 4–5
Fortune Book Club, 138
Fowlkes, Pat, 137
Fred Friendly Award, 143
Fremont-Smith, Eliot, 87

Frenzel, Bill, 149

Friday Lunch, Brookings Institution, 126

Frost, David, 135

Fundraising dinners, Eisenhower's speech, 41–42

Gaddafi, Muammar, 145

Garment, Len, 116, 172

The Gatekeepers (Whipple), 23

Geidt, Christopher, 174

Gender identification, classroom journalism exercise, 174–75

George Washington University, 176

Gergen, David, 167

Germany, Hess's military service, 17–18

Gerrity, Jessica, 143

Gettysburg College, 44

Ginsburg, Marty, 166, 167

Ginsburg, Ruth Bader, 166–68, *168*

"Give me a week" comment, Eisenhower's, 31–32

Globe Democrat, 81

"Gloomdoggle" invention, 40

Goldberg, Arthur, 82

Goldfine, Bernard, 3

Goldwater, Barry, 30, 75, 76

Good Morning, Chicago, 80

Goodpaster, Andrew, 19, 24, 33

Gordon, Kermit, 124, 126, 135

Gore, Al, 143, 144

Gore, Tipper, 144

Governing New York City (Kaufman), 127

Governmental Studies program, Brookings Institution, 126–29, 150, 163–64

The Government/Press Connection: Press Officers and Their Offices (Hess), 141–42

Grades, presidential, 46–47

Graff, Henry F., 78

Grant, Ulysses S., 118

Gray, Gordon, 26

Great Depression years, 7–8

Greece conference, 176

Green room, television, 88

Greenstein, Fred, 19

Grey, Lady Jane, 22

Gridiron Dinners, 36, 68

Griswold, Erwin, 167

Hagerty, James, 19, 20, 21–22, 25, 147

Haig, Alexander, 146

Haldeman, Bob: Nixon's presidential campaign, 69; scrapping of Mazo/Hess book, 77; staff management, 102; and Stone's movie, 172; Watergate scandal, 134, 135; Youth Conference, 110, 113–14

Haldeman, Jo, 134

Hall, Len, 75

Hamburg, Eric, 172

Hanford, Liddy, 100

Harding, Warren G., 52

Harlow, Bryce, 24, 25, 34, 52–53, 95

Harper & Row, 76–77

Harr, Karl, 22

Harriman, Averell, 97, 127, 131
Harriman, Edward, 131
Harvard Business School, 132
Harvard Summer News, 85, *86*
Harvard University, 82, 145–46,
 170–71
Hats in the Ring (Moos and Hess),
 14, 76, 88
Havens, Shirley Jean, 41–42
Health, Education, and Welfare
 (HEW), 101–02
Heatter, Gabriel, 7
Helsinki conference, 176
Herblock cartoon, 37
Herter, Christian, 20
Hess, Beth, 155, *157,* 166, 168,
 173–74, 180
Hess, Charles, 7–8, 76, 120, 129
Hess, Florence, 6, 7, 40
Hess, Jamie, 97, 118, 120
Hess, Stephen (overview): child-
 hood/youth, 6–10; college years,
 5–6, 10–16; early post-college
 work, 16–17; family background,
 6–8; military service, 3, 17–18.
 See also Bookmaking topics,
 Hess's; Brookings Institution,
 Hess's position; Eisenhower,
 Dwight D. (and administration);
 Nixon *entries*
"The Hess Report," 143
"Hibernating elephant" phrase, 37
Hickel, Walter, 146
The Hidden Hand Presidency (Green-
 stein), 19
Hiestand, Edgar, 62

Hoff, Philip, 170
Ho-Ho-Kus, New Jersey, 16
Holbrooke, Richard, 149
Hollywood Foreign Press Associa-
 tion, 143
Homan, Richard, 91
Home Rule Act, District of Colum-
 bia, 130
Hoover, J. Edgar, 74, 112
Hopkins, Anthony, 172–73
Hopkins Women's Republican
 Club, 14
Horn, Steve, 51
House of Representatives, U.S., 41,
 53, 104, 136, 141, 160. *See also*
 Congress, U.S.; Senate, U.S.
Human Events, 117
Humor, 14, 21, 39, 66–67
Humphrey, Hubert, 5–6, 14, 16,
 90, 91
Humphrey George, 19
Hurst, Charles, 108, 109
Hutchins, Robert, 10

Impeachment article, Nixon, 136
Inaugural address, Trump's, 180
Inauguration planning, 151
Inland Steel Company, 26
Innocent Until Nominated (Macken-
 zie), 150
Institute for International Econom-
 ics, 149
Institute for Policy Studies, 79
Institute of Politics, 82, 145–46,
 170–71
Integrity (Krogh), 135

International News & Foreign Correspondents, 142
Interstate Highway System, 46
Interview Award, 143
Iowa State University, 131
Israel, 160
Israel bond rally, 67

Javits, Jacob, 117–18
Jerusalem lectures, 176
John Birch Society, 62
Johns Hopkins University, 3, 5–6, 13–16
Johnson, Andrew, 47
Johnson, Lyndon Baines (and administration), 74–75, 83, 124, 127
Jones, Alex, 145
Jory, Victor, 66
Journalism Quarterly, 76

Kalb, Bernard, 145
Kalb, Marvin, 145, 156
Kaltenborn, H. V., 7
Kampelman, Max, 5–6
Kaplan, Milton, 76, 164–65
Karnow, Stanley, 156
Katzmann, Robert, 167
Kaufman, Herbert, 127
Keene, Daniel, 170
Kelley, Kitty, 114
Kennedy, Bobby, 75, 81
Kennedy, Jacqueline (later Onassis), 82, 170–71
Kennedy, John F. (and administration): assassination and after-

math, 73–75; Cuban missile crisis, 70; election of, 35, 87–88; Gordon appointments, 124; inaugural address, 180; job offer to Hess, 51; and Nixon's gubernatorial campaign, 60–61; staffers characterized, 26, 81; Supreme Court nomination, 67; transition planning, 26, 147
Kennedy, Teddy, 81
Kennedy School of Government, 82, 145–46, 170
Kerensky, Alexander, 10
Keyes, Paul, 66–68, 69, 73, 74
Khrushchev, Nikita, 22, 23, 71
Killian, James, 26
King, Larry, 88
King, Martin Luther Jr., 89, 130
Kinsley, Michael, 137–38
Kirkpatrick, Jeane, 176
Kissinger, Henry, 83, 95, 161
Kistiakowsky, George, 24
Klein, Herb, 69, 72
Knauer, Virginia, 100
Knight, Goodwin, 61
Knowland, Bill, 61
Koppel, Ted, 156
Krevsky, Elizabeth, 144
Kristof, Nick, 142–43
Krogh, Egil "Bud," 134–35
Kuchel, Thomas, 51–52
Kupcinet, Irv, 88
Kup's Show, 88

Ladies' Home Journal, 83–85
Lafayette Square, fence story, 98

Laird, Mel, 31

Lamb, Bernard, 16

Lambeau, Curly, 67

Landon, Alf, 7

Larson, Arthur, 3, 36–37

LaRue, Mr., 133

"Last press conference," Nixon's, 71–72

Laugh-In, Rowan & Martin's, 66, 67

Lawrence, Jacob, 98

Lawrence, Jill, 179

Leaks typology, 142

Lee, Sir Henry, 173

Lehman, Herbert, 5

Lehrer, Jim, 132

Lennon, John, 109

Levitt, Heidi, 172

Lewis, Flora, 113

Light, Paul C., 150

Lincoln, Abraham, 72, 180

Lincoln Week, 80

Lindsay, James, 162

Lindsay, John, 89

Litt, David, 35

The Little Book of Campaign Etiquette (Hess), 163–64

Live from Capitol Hill! Studies of Congress and the Media (Hess), 141

Livingston, Rose, 6

Lockheed, 80

Lodge, Henry Cabot, 34–35, 41, 89

Los Angeles Times Syndicate, 58, 59

Lovenheim, Sarah, 144

Lowenstein, Allard, 170

Lubin, Nathaniel, 144

MacArthur, Douglas, 19, 34, 37

MacDonald, Jeannette, 66

Mackenzie, G. Calvin, 150

MacLaury, Bruce, 145

Macmillan, Harold, 21

Macmillan (publisher), 76

MacNeil, Robert, 132

MacNelly, Jeff, 164

Magruder, Jeb, 134

Major, John, 173

Make-A-Wish Foundation, 162

The Making of the President (White), 73

Manchester, William, 147

Mann, Tom, 128

Mardian, Mr., 133

Margolis, Rita, 7

Marlow, Lynda, 144

Marshall, Thurgood, 167

Martin, Judith, 164

Mathews, John, 113

Mathis, Johnny, 66

Matthews, Chris, 52

Mayer, Jean, 103

Mazo, Earl, 77, 87

M'Bow, Amadou-Mahtar, 159

McCaffree, Mary Jane, 27

McCarthy, Joe, 90

McClendon, Sarah, 21–22

McCormick, Ken, 73

McGinniss, Joe, 67–68

McMillin, Bo, 39

McPhee, Roemer, 44

McPherson, Harry, 16

Media. *See* News media, Hess's in-
volvement; Television broadcasts,
Hess's involvement
The Media and the War on Terrorism
(Hess and Kalb), 158
Meese, Edwin, 148
Mellon, Richard, 4
Mencken, H. L., 10–11
Merriam, Bob, 33
Mess, Staff, 24, 25, 53
Michiko, Princess, 28
Military-industrial complex speech,
Eisenhower's, 36, 46
Military service, Hess's, 3, 17–18
Miller, William, 91
"Miss Manners," 164
Mitchell, Jim, 51
Mitchell, John, 133, 165
Mohr, Charles H., 31
Montgomery, Robert, 24
Moore, Constance, 66
Moore, Jonathan, 145, 170
Moos, Charley, 14
Moos, Malcolm: in academic life,
13–14, 16; in Baltimore politics,
14, 16; book publishing, 14, 76,
88; hiring of Hess, 3–4; Nixon's
presidential campaign, 34;
speechwriting processes, 35–37,
39, 40
Moos, Tracey, 40
Morgan, Dennis, 66
Morison, Samuel Eliot, 170
Morrow, E. Frederic, 27
Morse, Max (earlier Moskowitz),
6–7

Morton, Thurston, 57
Moskowitz, Belle, 6
Moskowitz, Henry, 6
The Mouse That Roared (movie), 21
Movie watching, Eisenhower's,
20–21
Moynihan, Daniel Patrick, 82, 95–
101, 135, 139, 147, 166–67, 171
Moynihan, Liz, 82, 171
Mueller, Fritz, 58
Muskie, Edmund, 94
My Governance Award, 143
My Old Man (Major), 174

NAACP, 6
Nader, Ralph, 100
Nast, Thomas, 97, 133
Nathan, Richard, 128
The Nation, 113
National Academy of Public Ad-
ministration, 149
National Endowment for the Hu-
manities, 116
National Gallery of Art, 97–98
National Observer, 94
National Press Club, 67, 164
National Public Radio, 143
NATO, 11, 24
Navy Department, 19, 24
NBC television, 144
Nelson-Atkins Museum of Art, 159
Nessen, Ron, 162
New Leader, 16
The New Republic, 118, 138
News media, Hess's involvement:
bookmaking about, 140–46, 158;

Brookings panels after September
11 attacks, 156, 158; in campaign
etiquette book, 163–64; civics
education columns, 175; class-
room exercise, 174–75
News media, Hess's involvement.
See also Television broadcasts,
Hess's involvement; *specific
media, e.g., New York Times*
Newsweek, 179–80
Newswork books, Hess's, 141–45
New Yorker, 79, 180
New York Herald Tribune, 87–88
New York Republican Committee,
12
New York Times: foreign correspon-
dents' stories, 142–43; in gender-
identification exercise, 174–75; in
Hess family home, 7
New York Times (article topics):
Agnew's speech, 91; Avedon's
photography, 172; books by Hess,
78, 79, 87; Brookings Institution,
123; Conference on Children,
106; gloomdoggle speech, 41;
Humanities chair nomination,
117; obituaries, 27, 158; presiden-
tial campaigns, 6
New York Times Book Review, 78
Nichter, Luke, 113
Nielson, Aksel, 42
Nigeria, 175
Nixon, Julie, 69, 83–85
Nixon, Pat, 63
Nixon, Richard M.: at 1952 national
convention, 12–13; Buchanan

hiring, 80; Eisenhower's press
conference, 32; going-away
ceremony for Hess, 118–20; and
Kennedy assassination, 74–75;
Krushchev meeting, 22; law
practice, 58, 73; presidential
campaigns, 32–33, 34, 41, 60,
87–95; Rockefeller meeting and
aftermath, 30–31; staff members
characterized, 59; and Stone's
movie, 172; as vice-president,
57–58; and World Affairs Council debate, 83; writing projects
with Hess, 58–59, 80–81
Nixon, Richard M. (administration of): Conference on Children, 102–09; Conference on
Youth, 102–03, 109–14; "good
news" story, 175; HEW staffing
changes, 101–02; Humanities
chair position, 116–18; inauguration music, 151; Moynihan's
urban affairs work, 95–101; staff
mess seating, 25; transition planning, 147; Watergate scandal,
131–36
Nixon, Richard M. (gubernatorial campaign): compared to
presidential campaigns, 62–63;
context of state politics, 61–62;
debate, 68–69; defeat factors,
69–71; and his presidential campaign, 60–61; post-defeat letter
from Hess, 72–73; press relations, 71–72; telethons, 64, 66;
whistle-stop tour, 63–64, *65*

Nixon (Mazo & Hess), 77, *78*, 87, 88
Nolan, Lloyd, 66
Northrup, Sandy, 165
Novak, Bob (*Crossfire* host), 137–38
Novak, Robert (*Washington Post* columnist), 91

Obama, Barack, 35, 150–51
Obama, Michelle, 98
Obermayer, Herman, 167–68
Oishi, Gene, 93
Okun, Arthur, 124, 126
Onassis, Jacqueline Kennedy, 82, 170–71
Oprah (Kelley), 114
Organizing the Presidency (Hess), 138
Osborne, John, 118, 138
Oswald, Lee Harvey, 145

Paar, Jack, 66
Pappas, Ike, 145
Park proposal, Nixon administration, 99
Parsons, Ann, 54
Pasternak, Alan, 10
Paton, Alan, 161
Patterson, Brad, 34
Payne, John, 66
PBS television, 132, 144–45, 165
Pechman, Joe, 126
Pell, Claiborne, 117
Pentagon Papers, 135
Percy, Charles, 28, 30
Perkins, Anthony, 88

Perkins, Rod, 30
Perry, George, 126
Perry, James, 94
Persons, Wilton (Jerry), 23, 25, 26, 33, 43, 53
Peterson, Arthur, 117
Pew Charitable Trusts, 163
Pfiffner, James P., 139
Philadelphia Inquirer, 136
Philip, Prince, 22
Phrase and Fable, 8, 10
Pinkett, Flaxie, 129–30
Platform Committee, Republican, 28, 30–31, 43, 158–59
Poggioli, Sylvia, 143
Policymaking for Social Security (Derthick), 127
Political cartooning, Hess's books about, 76, 164–66
A Political Education (McPherson), 16
Pomfret, John, 142
Population density speech, Agnew's, 92
The Presidential Campaign (Hess), 128–29
Presidential Medal of Freedom, 6
Presley, Elvis, 3
Price, John, 98
Price, Ray, 59
Procter & Gamble, 53
The Professor and the President (Hess), 95, 101
Progressive Party, 6, 13
The Public Papers of the Presidents, 52

Quinn, Sandy, 62, 72

Racism, 26–27, 43, 89, 90, 93, 161–62
Raddatz, Martha, 143–44
Randall, Clarence, 26, 51
Random House, 76
Rapoport, Roger, 113
Ravitch, Richard, 40
Ray, Robert, 158
Reagan, Ronald (and administration), 62, 89, 139, 145, 148, 159
Redford, Robert, 151
Rehnquist, William, 167
Rehnquist (Obermayer), 167–68
Reichley, James, 128
The Republican Establishment (Hess and Broder), 61, 77, 83
Republican Party: Hess's book about, 61, 77, 83; "hibernating elephant" phrase, 37; National Committee activity, 3–4, 16–17, 19, 53, 56–57, 148; National Conventions, 10–11, 85, 130, 159; Platform Committee work, 28, 30–31, 43, 158–59
Reuters, 136
Rhodehamel, John, 44
Richardson, Elliot, 111, 136
Rickover, Hyman, 168, 170
Rimel, Rebecca, 163, 164
Riots, urban, 89, 100
Rivers, William, 140
Rivlin, Alice, 126
RN (Nixon), 135
Roberts, Ellin, 73

Roberts, Victoria, 180
Robertson, Nan, 106
Robeson, Paul, 13
Rockefeller, Nelson, 30, 41, 60, 83, 89
Rockefeller Foundation, 144
Rocky Mountain News, 111
Rogers, Bill (Eisenhower cabinet member), 58
Rogers, William P. (Nixon cabinet member), 175
Rolling Stone, 113
Rome, Harold, 8
Romero, Cesar, 66
Romney, George, 60
Roosevelt, Franklin D., 8, 19, 124, 151, 156, 180
Roosevelt, Theodore, 4, 6, 19, 102
Roosevelt Room, White House, 21
Rosapepe, Jim, 104–05
Rosten, Leo, 140
Rousselot, John, 62
Rowan & Martin's Laugh-In, 66, 67
Ruby, Jack, 145
Run Silent, Run Deep (Beach), 24
Ruth, Babe, 7
Rux, Karen, 112

Safire, Bill, 59, 118, 135
Safire, Helene, 135
Salinger, Pierre, 147
Saturday Evening Post, 58, 59
Saturday Review, 79, 113
Schlesinger, Arthur M. Jr., 47
Schlesinger, Arthur M. Sr., 46–47
Schlesinger, Robert, 59

Schorr, Daniel, 156
Schultze, Charles, 126, 162
Scott, Randy, 58
Scranton, William, 60, 160
Sears, John, 90, 93, 172
Secret Service, 20, 53, 56, 84–85
Security speech, Eisenhower's,
    39–40
Seeger, Pete, 109
The Selling of the President (McGinniss), 67–68
Senate, U.S.: bookmaking about,
    141; Bricker Amendment, 5–6;
    confirmation processes, 150, 167;
    election outcomes, 41; Humanities chair position, 116–18; from
    Nixon administration staff, 100;
    speechwriting for Kuchel, 51–52;
    UN delegation, 160; Watergate
    hearings, 132, 135–36
September 11 attacks, aftermath,
    156, 158
Seward, William, 72
Shell, Joseph, 62
Shipman, Claire, 144
Shorenstein Center on Media, Politics and Public Policy, 145
Simon, Bob, 142
60 Minutes, 144
Six Crises (Nixon), 59
Smith, Alfred E., 6
Smith, Anna Devere, 175
Smith, Gene, 59
Smith, James Allen, 123–24
Smithsonian, 97–98
Snyder, Howard, 34

Sochi conference, 175–76
Sohmer, Art, 92
South Africa, 161–62
Soviet Union, 22, 23, 68, 70–71
The Speechwriter (Swaim), 59
Staats, Elmer, 149
Stahl, Leslie, 144
Stassen, Harold, 26
State Department, U.S.: Agnew's
    resignation letter, 95; Carter's appointee, 150; in Executive Office
    Building, 19; Kalb's resignation
    story, 145; and September 11
    attacks, 156, 158; and United
    Nations, 160, 161–62
State of the Union address, Eisenhower's, 43
Steel industry, Truman conflict, 26
Steiger, Bill, 79
Steiner, Fay, 44
Steiner, Gilbert Y., 109, 127
Stephens, Tom, 25
Stevenson, Adlai, 74, 75
Stone, Oliver, 172–73
Storm, Gale, 66
Strauss, Robert, 53
Stuart, Gilbert, 118
The Sunday Times, 88
Sundquist, James, 127
Supreme Court, U.S., 26, 43, 67,
    136, 166–68
Swaim, Barton, 59
Sweden, C-SPAN discussion, 176
Swisher, Carl, 13
Syracuse University, 174–75

Taft, Robert, 11

Talbott, Strobe, 145

Tall Story (Fonda), 88

Teachers College, District of Columbia, 129

Telethons, Nixon's gubernatorial campaign, 64, 66

Television broadcasts, Hess's involvement: bookmaking about, 143–45; coverage of Watergate hearings, 132–34; interviews on, 80, 88, 136–38; production process, 165. *See also* News media, Hess's involvement

Tenpas, Kathryn Dunn, 176

Texas, vote fraud accusation, 87

Thank-you note to Eisenhower, Hess's, 47

Think tank, defined, 123

Thomas, Alma, 98

Through Their Eyes: Foreign Correspondents in the United States, 143

Tin Lizzie image, 40

Tkach, Walter, 22

Tonight show, 66

Trachtenberg, Stephen, 176

Transition periods, presidential, 146–51

Tree, Ronald, 173

Triton, USS, 25

Trolley riding, 8

Trudeau, Garry, 165

Trudeau, Pierre, 118

Truman, Harry, 14, 26, 34, 42, 63, 124, 127

Trump, Donald, 179–80

Tuck, Dick, 64

Tugwell, Rex, 138

Turkey, political cartoonists, 165

Tweed Ring cartoon, 133

Twentieth Century Fund, 131

The Ultimate Insiders: U.S. Senators in the National Media (Hess), 141

The Uncommon Reader (Bennett), 174

UNESCO, 159–60

The Ungentlemanly Art (Hess), 76, 164–65

Unger, Roberto, 176

United Nations, 110, 139, 159–62

United States Information Agency, 31

University of Chicago, 10

University of District of Columbia, 129–30

University of Minnesota, 16

University of Southern California, 176

UPI debate, Nixon's gubernatorial campaign, 68–69, 70

Urban Affairs Council, Nixon administration, 95–101, 147

USA Today, 143, 179

Vallée, Rudy, 66–67

Vance, Cyrus, 150

Vanocur, Sander, 32–33

Veneman, Jack, 102

Vest-pocket park proposal, Nixon administration, 99

Vietnam War, 83, 103, 109, 112

Villa Serbelloni, 144
Volunteer army idea, 83, 112
Vote fraud series, Mazo's, 87–88

Waldron, Agnes, 68
Wallace, Henry, 13
Wall Street Journal, 90, 174–75
Ward, Paul, 36
War Department, Executive Office Building, 19
War Industries Board, 123
Waring, Fred, 23
Washington, George, 4–5, 118
Washington, Walter, 106, *107,* 129
The Washington Correspondents (Rosten), 140
Washington Daily News, 40
Washington Post: in gender-identification exercise, 174–75; in Hess family home, 7
Washington Post (articles): Agnew, 91, 93; Children's Conference, 106, *107;* foreign correspondents' decision-making, 142; Iowa governor obituary, 158; Nixon administration, 104–05, 106, *107*
Washington Post Magazine, 109
The Washington Reporters (Hess), 141
Washington Technical Institute, 129
Watergate scandal, 131–36, 165
Wedemeyer, Albert C., 34
Weisman, Steven, 142
Welch, Robert, 62
Welliver, Judson, 52

West, Cornel, 176
West, Darrell, 128
West Point, 33
What Do We Do Now? (Hess), 151
Whatever Happened to the Washington Reporters 1978–2012 (Hess), 144
Wheaton, Anne, 27
When the Cheering Stopped (Smith), 59
Whipple, Chris, 23
Whistle-stop tour, Nixon's gubernatorial campaign, 63–64, *65*
Whitaker, John, 80
White, Bryon "Whizzer," 67
White, Theodore, 73, 85
White House Conference on Children, 103–09
White House Conference on Children and Youth, 102–103
White House Conference on Hunger, 103
White House Conference on Youth, 102–03, 109–14
White House Ghosts (Schlesinger), 59
White House Staff Book, 1953–1961, 27
Whitman, Ann, 22, 27, 56
Wilkinson, Bud, 99
Williams, Camilla, 28
Williams, Ralph, 35, 36, 44
Wills, Sir David, 173
Wilson, Charles, 19
Wilson, Henry, 118
Wilson, Woodrow, 59, 118
Winfrey, Oprah, 114, 116

Witcover, Jules, 90

Wolman, Abel, 168, 170

Woodruff, Judy, 144–45

Woods, James, 172

Woods, Rose Mary, 62, 70, 74, 77

Woodward, C. Vann, 117

World Affairs Council, 83

World Telegram, 7

World War II, 7–8, 11, 173

Writing projects, Hess's: about D. Eisenhower and J. Nixon, 83–85; with Nixon, 58–59, 80–81; school magazine, 8, 10; Washington newsletter, 56–57, 58. *See also* Bookmaking topics, Hess's

York, Mary Nell, 113

Youth poverty programs, Nixon administration, 99

Ziegler, Ron, 62, 72, 172

Zorthian, Barry, 156